W9-AED-443

Mrs. Caroline Norton

From a J. H. Robinson engraving of the
Thomas Carrick portrait

Reproduced by kind permission of the British Museum

The Letters
of Caroline Norton
to Lord Melbourne

Edited by

JAMES O. HOGE *and* CLARKE OLNEY

DOWNS JONES LIBRARY
HUSTON - TILLOTSON COLLEGE

*Ohio State
University Press*

PR5112
N5
A845
1974

Copyright © 1974 by the Ohio State University Press
All rights reserved
Manufactured in the United States of America

Library of Congress Cataloging in Publication Data

Norton, Caroline Sheridan, 1808–1877.
The letters of Caroline Norton to Lord Melbourne.

Includes bibliographical references.
1. Norton, Caroline Sheridan, 1808–1877 — Correspondence. 2. Melbourne,
William Lamb, 2d Viscount, 1779–1848. I. Melbourne, William Lamb, 2d Vis-
count, 1779–1848. II. Hoge, James O., ed. III. Olney, Clarke, 1901– ed. IV.
Title.
PR5112.N5A845   1974   821'.8 [B]   74–12344
                          ISBN   0-8142-0208-X

$10.75

until of Texas Press
"General Fund"

12-7-76

62968

Dedication

Cecil Y. Lang
and James O. Hoge, Sr.
(1899–1966)

Contents

Illustrations

Lord Melbourne in 1838
From the painting by Sir George Hayter
Reproduced by kind permission of Lord Brocket

Preface

CAROLINE NORTON wrote the first of the letters in this collection in July, 1831, when she was twenty-three and in the first flush of her enchantment with William Lamb, second viscount Melbourne, then home secretary in Earl Grey's cabinet. After years of Tory ascendancy, which he passed in enforced leisure at Brocket Hall, Melbourne at fifty-two was nearing the apex of his career, bidding at last to fulfill the promise of his enormous intellectual capacity and his political acumen. The last letter, which Mrs. Norton wrote in December, 1844, reflects the final phase of their relationship. Melbourne's decade of political authority had ended, and he was back at Brocket, neglected and ill. The feeling implicit in Mrs. Norton's final letters is that of an old friend, with pity for the infirmity and loneliness of the man who had known her admiration, her love, her anger, and her contempt and who had through the years been privy to her most intimate thoughts and to her innumerable tribulations.

These letters have hitherto been inaccessible to the biographers of Melbourne and Caroline Norton. They constitute a small part of the extensive accumulation of records and papers relating to the Cowper and Lamb (Melbourne) families that until 1953 were kept at Panshanger, near Hertford, the country seat of the earls Cowper until 1905 when the title became extinct. In 1953 Panshanger was demolished, the salable contents of the house disposed of, and a century or more of papers were deposited in the Hertford County Record Office. Professor Clarke Olney of the University of Georgia was subsequently granted access to the Panshanger Collection in 1954. Professor Olney recognized the Caroline Norton letters as a treasure trove of new information about Mrs. Norton and Lord Melbourne and their controversial relationship, including the criminal conversation suit of George Chapple Norton against Melbourne. After securing microfilms of all the Norton letters, with the kind assistance of Lady Monica Salmond, legatee at that time of the Cowper Papers, Olney worked at editing and arranging them; but he died leaving his projected edition unfinished. Four years ago the heirs of Professor Olney presented the Clarke Olney Papers to the Special Collections Department of the University of Georgia Libraries; and it is through the generosity of the Olney heirs and of the University of Georgia Libraries in kindly allowing me to use their property, that I have been able to complete this edition.

The merits of these letters individually and as a collection are clear. Caroline Sarah (Sheridan) Norton was a notable literary figure in the nineteenth century, particularly during the 1830s and 1840s. A granddaughter of Richard Brinsley Sheridan, she inherited much of his literary gift, including a remarkable facility in composition. Although her works by now have been largely forgotten, in her day Mrs. Norton was widely read and highly regarded. She was constantly involved in one literary project or another, and her output of both poetry and fiction, in the face of all the distractions that disturbed her career, is proof both of the ease with which she wrote and of her compulsion for literary expression. By the time she was twenty-one, she had published two books of poetry; and she subsequently published four more volumes, as well as many short miscellaneous poems in the *Edinburgh Review,* in Bulwer-Lytton's *New Monthly,* and in her own *La Belle Assemblée and Court Magazine,* which she edited from 1832 until 1837. When *The Dream* appeared in 1840, Hartley Coleridge was so impressed with the tender grace and elegance of that wistful, romantic poem that he wrote a review in which he termed her "the Byron of modern poetesses" and placed her first in a list of ten British poetesses, of whom Elizabeth Barrett was the second. Though she was best known for her poetry, Mrs. Norton also published three novels and two novellas, all of which bear the stamp of her notoriously tragic marriage; and she edited several periodicals of the "keepsake" variety, in addition to *La Belle Assemblée*.

The collection is significant for its candid disclosure of Caroline Norton's immediate reactions both to events in her always tempestuous personal life and to contemporary political transactions, particularly as they involved Lord Melbourne. The letters contribute to our understanding of Mrs. Norton herself, and of course they shed further light on the nature of her friendship with Melbourne, a subject of speculation ever since George Norton entered suit for damages in an adultery action in May, 1836.

But in addition to their biographical interest and their statement about the relationship of two eminent Victorians, the letters are readable in their own right. Virtually every letter testifies to the composition of a professional writer. Mrs. Norton's language is both passionate and learned, and she is always spontaneous, frank, and vivid in her expression of personal feelings or in her chronicle of domestic life in London at her own home in Storey's Gate or at her sister's home in pastoral Wiltshire. Of all her literary contemporaries Mrs. Norton drew highest praise for her conversational powers, and the urbanity, good humor, and daring unconventionality that informed her speech are evident in her letters to Melbourne. Her flirtatious letters are charged with spirited intelligence and with a uniquely Sheridan wit. And when she found Melbourne blameworthy, she wrote withering criticism, denouncing what she saw as indolence, cowardice, or infidelity.

The supreme virtue in letter-writing is spontaneity. Caroline Norton wrote these letters to the man she loved and respected above all others, and she intended them only for his eyes. The fact that they were undoubtedly not written with an eye to

xiii

ultimate publication (as many eighteenth- and nineteenth-century letters were) adds to their importance as an authentic record of her thoughts and feelings. The letters of Melbourne to Mrs. Norton have not been similarly assembled, and it is likely that most of them have not been preserved. Nonetheless, several have been reproduced in scattered sources, and from these it would appear that most of his side of the correspondence, at least after Norton's initial accusation, consisted of attempts to offer her sympathy and advice, while discreetly disengaging himself from her affections. Much of what he had to say to her is implicit in Mrs. Norton's letters to him.

One of the principal problems in dealing with letters of this sort — written with no idea of future disclosure — is the matter of chronology. Mrs. Norton was often writing under emotional pressure, and she seldom bothered to date her letters. As a result, internal evidence and a knowledge of concurrent events have determined their most likely order. The letters fall naturally into three main groups: (1) those written in 1831 during their early and carefree relationship; (2) those written shortly before and shortly after the June, 1836, trial; and (3) those written during their later, more serene friendship, which lasted until Melbourne's death in 1848. It is evident that the letters in this collection do not constitute all those written by Mrs. Norton to Lord Melbourne. We cannot know of those letters that he chose to destroy; and it is altogether possible that some of those he preserved were later removed or discarded during the century or more they reposed in the Cowper family archives.

In editing these letters, I have observed several principles:

1. My first concern has been to present the texts of these letters with an absolute minimum of change. In order to do justice to the individuality of Caroline Norton and to preserve an authentic record of the disheveled artlessness of her character, as well as the emotional stress under which she often wrote, I

have retained all of her verbal idiosyncracies. Her ampersands, misspellings, and inconsistencies in spelling have been permitted to stand, along with incomplete or ramshackle sentences, run-on paragraphs, lower-case letters that should be capitals, and misplaced, incorrect, or incomplete punctuation. Titles of books not underlined by Mrs. Norton are reproduced in roman type. Corrections or additions essential for clarity are enclosed in the usual editorial square brackets.

2. In all cases I have preserved Mrs. Norton's abbreviations, including the abbreviated names of people. If an abbreviation is cryptic without expansion, the remainder of the word is provided in square brackets.

3. I have reproduced the dates and addresses of all letters just as they appear in the originals, adding square brackets when any part of the date or address is an editorial conjecture.

4. I have used ellipses to indicate the omission of the few words or sentences that I have judged so awkward or confusing as to hinder the reader. All ellipses are my own.

5. While trying to keep both the number and bulk of my annotations to a minimum, I have attempted to make Mrs. Norton's letters as comprehensible to the present reader as they would have been to her correspondent. Usually I have identified only at their first occurence unfamiliar persons, places, events, quotations, and publications, and I have noted what I could not identify.

6. Contrary to Mrs. Norton's regular practice, the paragraph indention at the opening of each letter has been omitted, and the headings and signatures to the letters have been italicized throughout. Single and double underscorings have been rendered uniformly in italics; no attempt has been made to preserve the distinction between the two forms of emphasis.

It is my pleasure to acknowledge those who have assisted me. Clearly I owe an unparalleled debt to Professor Olney, who

Introduction

CAROLINE NORTON'S FATHER, Tom Sheridan, the only son of Richard Brinsley Sheridan and his first wife, Elizabeth Linley, died in 1817, when Caroline was nine years old. Sheridan left little to support his widow and seven children, but the Sheridan social status was a powerful asset. By utilizing her name and acquaintances to best advantage, Mrs. Sheridan was able to introduce Caroline and her sisters, Helen and Georgiana, into the small and influential inner circle of fashionable London society. All three Sheridan girls were beautiful and talented, and it is a tribute to their personal fascination, as much as to their mother's designs, that they were successful in earning the approval of the most elevated element of masculine London in the late 1820s.

As George Meredith contended, "A witty woman is a treasure; a witty Beauty is a power."[1] Caroline, "brunette with magnificent, expressive eyes that were her most striking feature,"[2] was particularly admired, both for her classical Linley beauty and for her intellectual abilities. She had already established herself as a popular poet; "her conversation and her Irish wit sparkled"; she played, sang, and was a talented mimic; and "her free, almost bold manners" amused and delighted most of her male acquaintances, though her impudent talk and behavior shocked some of her more staid contemporaries.[3] In 1827 Emily, Lady Cowper, the sister of William and Frederick Lamb, wrote to Frederick about the Sheridan girls:

> The Sheridans are much admired but are strange girls, swear and say all sorts of odd things to make the men laugh. I am surprised so sensible a Woman as Mrs. Sheridan should let them go on so. I suppose she cannot stop the old blood coming out. They are remarkably good looking . . . and certainly clever.[4]

But cleverness, as Meredith observed, "is an attribute of the selecter missionary lieutenants of Satan. . . . The wary stuff their ears, the stolid bid her best sayings rebound on her reputation."[5] In 1828, shortly after Caroline married George Norton, Henry Edward Fox (afterward Lord Holland) recorded in his *Journal* several "strange stories," related to him by Lord Wriothesley Russell, about Caroline and her eccentricities. Fox thought her habits, particularly her flirtatious behavior with men, "dangerous and indecent for so young a woman," but he admitted that her verve and audacity had made her the current fashion and that people admired her prodigiously.[6] Even Alice Acland, her biographer, who parries virtually every attack upon Caroline's reputation, cites the "thoughtless unconventionality" her heroine displayed both before and after her fateful marriage in June, 1827.

The younger brother of Fletcher Norton, third baron Grantley, of Wonersh Park, George Chapple Norton was a barrister by profession, but an inactive one. As a younger son, and brother and heir of a peer, he required some occupation, and in 1826 the Tories had him elected to Parliament to represent Guildford, the county town of Surrey. He proved a stupid and indolent politician, however, more concerned with his own pecuniary interests than with the obligations of his position; and his brief parliamentary career ended in 1830, when he lost his seat in the general election that followed the death of George IV. Caroline first met Norton at the age of sixteen, when she was attending school at a small establishment in Shalford, near Wonersh. When they next encountered each other in London three years later, Norton found himself in love with Caroline and determined to marry her. She was not in the least attracted to him, but, realizing the necessity of marriage to someone of wealth and family, she allowed herself to be drawn into a *mariage de convenance* with a man in whom she (or the world) would find little to admire or respect.

From the beginning the union was disastrous. Caroline's talents, her intelligence, and her ardent, untamed vitality were completely incompatible with the dull, stubborn, vulgar, and sometimes brutal character of her husband. She was just the type of woman to fascinate the London intelligentsia, and she was on admirable terms with such luminaries as Dickens, Henry Taylor, Thomas Moore, Abraham Hayward, Harrison Ainsworth, Benjamin Haydon, and the elderly and wealthy Samuel Rogers, who did much to encourage Caroline's entrée into scholarly circles and to broaden her literary acquaintance. Often she dined, without her husband, at Rogers's or at Hayward's, delighting everyone with her informed, witty conversation and holding her own with some of the best minds in England. When Charles Sumner, the Boston jurist, met Caroline at a dinner party in the late 1830s, he marveled at her many accomplishments, particularly her speech, which, he wrote, joined "the grace and ease of the woman with a strength and skill of which any man might well be proud."[7] Unlike Fanny Kemble, Lady Holland, and other female literati, Caroline coupled intellectual prowess with a charming and engaging femininity. At dinner parties she often closed the evening with several songs, some of her own composition, and her voice was thought to be quite as perfect as her wit.[8]

Caroline's immense popularity rankled the boorish Norton, whose own bad taste and slow manner discouraged the attention of fashionable society. Complacent and obtuse though he was, Norton was entirely aware of his wife's acceptance in circles closed to him, and much of his cruelty to Caroline was undoubtedly born of his frustration in attempting to cope with her obvious superiority. Disgusted by her husband's dullness, insensitivity, and idle selfishness, Caroline made no secret of her contempt for him. Of course in the early nineteenth century there was no legal recourse for a mismated wife — an injustice against which Caroline was later to wage incessant war. She, therefore, had no choice but to accept her unfortunate lot and look for solace in her sons, Fletcher (b. 1829), Brinsley (b. 1831), and William (b. 1833).

The animosity was exacerbated by their political alignments. The Nortons were high Tories, the Sheridans, Whigs to the core. In a time when political cleavages were acute, and political loyalties an integral part of social life, such a disparity would have threatened the stability of a more harmonious union. Caroline was headstrong and frank to a fault, and she offered no pretense of altering her Whig sympathies to pacify Norton. Instead, longing for political acceptance and influence, she flirted outrageously with the rising Whigs who came to her modest salon in Storey's Gate, located auspiciously near the Houses of Parliament. In 1832 Caroline was in the forefront of the campaign for the Reform Bill, and her tireless soliciting of Whig votes in the very presence of her Tory husband aroused an abiding resentment in the Norton family. Thereafter the Nortons treated Caroline with open hostility, neglecting no opportunity to abuse her directly or to encourage her husband's intolerance, and it was their interference in 1836 that precluded any chance of Norton's conciliation and thereby guaranteed the convergence of the twain.

At the time her acquaintance with Lord Melbourne began, in December, 1830, Caroline was already thoroughly disenchanted with Norton. Ironically, however, it was in her husband's behalf that she first communicated with his lordship. Although Norton had represented himself to Caroline as a man of considerable means, he had proved to be virtually penniless, and the couple had subsisted for three years on royalities from Caroline's publications. Norton desperately needed a job with a substantial income, and during the autumn of 1830 Caroline petitioned the home secretary and others in his behalf. Melbourne showed himself "in a most amiable light." When he was benevolently disposed, he did nothing by halves, and his kindness towards the Norton family did the greatest honor to his benevolent discrimination. He visited Caroline in Storey's Gate, and shortly thereafter Norton was appointed a magistrate in the metropolitan police courts, "a position which he retained with notable inefficiency, through all the difficulties that followed."[9]

Melbourne in 1830 was lonely and disconsolate. His wife, the celebrated Lady Caroline Lamb, best remembered for her tragicomic relationship with Lord Byron, had died two years before; and his relationship with Lady Branden of the Irish peerage was now largely a thing of the past.[10] As a widower, Melbourne had practiced a deliberate detachment in his personal life, avoiding any relationship that might disturb his official position or involve him in unwanted responsibilities. Nonetheless, feminine companionship had always been a necessity of his nature, and Caroline Norton, nearly thirty years his junior, amused and refreshed him. Like Byron's frolic Duchess of Fitz-Fulke, she "who loved *tracasserie,*/Began to treat him with some small *agacerie.*"[11] And her exhilarating warmth and spontaneity were perfect antidotes for the sad mistrust and cynicism that marred Melbourne's disposition. *En somme,* he found her altogether delightful, and he soon became her regular guest, calling every evening on the way home from his office to his lodgings in South Street.

Like Melbourne, Caroline was starved for real affection, and though her feelings toward him were at first partly filial, there is more than a trace of flirtation in the earliest letters she wrote him. For all his years, Melbourne was handsome and robust, and his superb intelligence and his position on the highest level of government and society could not have failed to attract a woman of Caroline's temperament.[12] From her girlhood Caroline had been fascinated by political intrigue, and she aspired to the kind of behind-the-scenes influence exercised by the great Whig ladies of the previous century, such as the duchess of Devonshire (the immortal Georgiana) and Viscountess Melbourne, Byron's confidante and the home secretary's mother. Melbourne was at Storey's Gate daily during the early 1830s, whether he saw Caroline alone or in the company of the artists, literary men, and other politicians who increasingly frequented her drawing room. [13] As his faith in her discretion and her intelligence grew more secure, Melbourne took Caroline into his most intimate confidence, and, when he formed his second cabinet in 1835, he enabled her to step into the kind of active political role she had always dreamed of. [14]

As Caroline busied herself with her ever expanding social, literary, and political activities, George Norton became increasingly resentful of a success that owed nothing to him. Certainly Caroline had never loved her husband, and she often gave him full benefit of her sharp tongue, scolding him for his indolence and his obtuseness and reminding him of her Sheridan superiority. Norton, for all his pathological selfishness, loved his wife after his fashion, but his jealousy and resentment were constantly inflamed by what his family said against her. His spinster sister Augusta and an elderly spinster cousin, Margaret Vaughan, were almost frenzied in their hatred of Caroline, and they pushed him to acts of irrational cruelty that he probably would not have committed without their insistence. After a violent scene in the summer of 1835, Caroline left Storey's Gate, ostensibly never to come back. But Norton had exclusive rights to the children, and Caroline was compelled to return to his house in order to live with her sons. She then lived in a state of unhappy truce with him until the following spring, when Norton decided on a step that would, he thought, punish his wife, and, at the same time, obtain for himself a considerable amount of money and advance his political fortunes with the Tories. In May, 1836, after some uncertainty as to whom in Caroline's circle of male friends he should move against, Norton formally accused his wife of adultery and entered suit for £10,000 damages in a criminal conversation action against Melbourne.

The relationship that Caroline and Melbourne had enjoyed

for more than five years was bound to excite suspicion, especially after his selection for the premiership, and their intimacy was a subject of town gossip long before the spring of 1836. Melbourne, and for that matter the entire Lamb family, had what Lord David Cecil terms an "amorous reputation"; and Caroline, "showily beautiful," aggressive, and "the opposite of prudish" in manner, was hardly the woman to disarm rumor.[15] When Norton filed his suit, London gossips accepted the justification of his charges as a foregone conclusion, and Caroline became the particular prey of scandal-mongering journals, which gave her story the fullest and most sensational exposure.[16] Strangely enough, Norton had never evidenced the slightest resentment of Melbourne before 1836. In fact he had always encouraged his wife's relationship with the prime minister, presumably hoping to retain his magistracy along with Melbourne's good favor. It is impossible to doubt that Norton's suspicions were aroused by his family and his Tory friends and that on their advice he decided to take advantage of his wife's indiscretions to obtain a divorce, as well as a fortune in damages. Norton's guardian, William Draper Best, first baron Wynford, very likely had a hand in devising the entire scheme, hoping the scandal would discredit Melbourne's government and bring about a Whig defeat. From what he subsequently admitted, it appears that Norton was never really convinced of a guilty relationship between his wife and Melbourne. Surely he was never seriously suspicious of Edward John Trelawny, Harrison Ainsworth, the duke of Devonshire, or others among Caroline's male friends whom he originally thought of charging. Though he may have ultimately persuaded himself that Caroline and Melbourne were lovers, he initially moved against the prime minister not for reasons of jealousy or honor but because he thought it financially and politically expedient to do so.

The trial on June 23 — which Dickens later caricatured in the breach of promise action of Bardell versus Pickwick — was surprisingly anticlimactic. Indeed, the evidence against Melbourne was "so trivial and the testimony so obviously corrupt" that the jury voted an acquittal without leaving the box. The public, shocked by the thin and shoddy case for the prosecution, generally approved of Melbourne's exoneration; the Whigs, of course, breathed more freely; and rumor correctly described the whole affair as "a bit of Tory skulduggery."[17] The biographers of both Mrs. Norton and Melbourne have also been quite willing to approve the jury's verdict. Alice Acland writes of their "romantic friendship" and their mental flirtation, and David Cecil cites Melbourne's repeated avowal, "on his honor as a peer," that his relations with Mrs. Norton had been innocent.[18]

One may, nonetheless, remain unconvinced. Obviously it is "as impossible now to prove that Caroline and Melbourne were or were not lovers as it was then."[19] But certainly in the letters collected here Caroline expressed emotions that exceed the bounds of friendship. There can be no doubt she loved Melbourne dearly. She said as much in a number of the letters she wrote him after the trial, when she felt he had deserted her. It is the tone of these scolding, reproachful letters, in particular, that suggests "the discarded mistress" rather than "the disappointed friend."[20]

Five days after the trial Melbourne's brother, Frederick Lamb (later Lord Beauvale), wrote to his sister Emily, expressing his relief at the verdict in language that hints at a less than absolute faith in its accuracy: *"Quel triomphe! J'ai ta lettre du 23. . . .* Don't let Wm think himself invulnerable for having got off again this time; no man's luck can go further." In the same letter Lamb also set down his sympathy for Mrs. Norton and his disgust at the "abomination" of exposing "the whole of a poor Woman's private and most interior life" to public inspection. "With a little protection" and support from the Lamb family, however, he felt she might in the future "do very well."[21] Unfortunately, however, Caroline did not do well at all. Melbourne emerged from the trial with little damage to his social position and none to his career, but the charge of adultery, despite the court's findings, tarnished Caroline's reputation irreparably. By the late 1830s her indiscreet wit and her general eccentricity were not regarded with the warm amusement of a single decade before. In any case, Victoria was on the throne, Melbourne in his heyday, and it is not altogether fanciful to see the young queen as a rival planet in the ascendant. Caroline was out of tune with the increasingly strict, censorious spirit of the day, and many Londoners found it easy to think the worst of a bold beauty living apart from her husband. Others who judged her innocent still thought it prudent to avoid social contact with so "questionable" a lady as Caroline Norton. A full ten years after the Melbourne scandal William Brookfield wrote to his mother that, although he believed Mrs. Norton "to be as entirely free from any impropriety as Miss Bates or Miss Harrison or Mrs. Best, — three as spotless virgins I should think as the chaste moon ever sees putting on their night caps," all the same he would "not approve of her as an intimate friend."[22]

Caroline's proved innocence in the action against Melbourne made it impossible for Norton to divorce her, but she continued to live apart from him, at first with her mother at Hampton Court and then with her uncle Charles Sheridan. Caroline was passionately maternal, and the enforced separation from her sons precluded the possibility of any real adjustment or peace of mind. Once the notoriety of the trial had subsided, she obtained a degree of readmittance to the social world through the agency of such prominent friends as Samuel Rogers, Lord Lansdowne, Lord Holland, and the duchess of Sutherland.[23] But even occasional access to her children depended entirely on her husband's compliance, and he procrastinated interminably, while the children remained in Scotland with his sister and brother-in-law, Sir Neil and Lady Menzies. Norton would agree to none of Caroline's proposals for visiting the boys, and his own proposals were always accompanied by awkward attempts to force his wife into a financial agreement favorable to himself, which would leave her utterly destitute.

Unable to sway a man, Caroline decided magnificently to persuade a government. In her despair over Norton's refusal to let her even see her children, she determined, in the autumn of 1836, to work for a change in the law that awarded the custody of infants solely to their fathers. Long a proponent of liberal Whig reform and a champion in verse of the deprived and the unjustly used, Caroline now had good reason for taking up the cause of women's rights. With the assistance of Abraham Hayward, she arranged for Serjeant Talfourd, a member of Parliament and junior counsel for Melbourne in the trial, to introduce to Commons a new Infant Custody Bill. On February 1, 1837, Talfourd gave notice of his bill, the first feminist legislation ever to come before Parliament. The bill was printed some two months later, and the second reading set for May 24. In the meantime, however, with characteristic inconsistency, Norton had promised to have the children brought home from Scotland on the condition that Caroline either forgive the past and return to him or else agree to a permanent financial settlement. Although she did not relish the thought of living with her husband again, Caroline was weary of fighting for access to her boys, and, encouraged by the prospect of immediate reunion with them, she consented to Norton's offer. In June, Talfourd withdrew his bill, probably at Caroline's direct request and certainly as a result of the favorable turn in her negotiations with Norton. The controversy of parliamentary debate on such a bill, intimately connected as it was with Caroline's name, would unquestionably have rekindled Norton's rancor and dashed all hopes of reconciliation.

Norton soon changed his mind, however, and again refused to recall the children from the Menzies's Rannoch Lodge. When she realized that her husband's offer had been the product of nothing more than a momentary whim, Caroline wrote him a desperate letter, expressing her amazement that "any human being should have the heart" so to abuse and play upon the sorrow of another: "You said my children should come! It is most barbarous to deceive me after all . . . to renew my hope, my anxiety, and my restlessness, only to destroy me by inches, as you are doing! I can give you no worse reproach than this: — I really *did* believe you."[24] Finally in mid-June the boys actually were permitted to come to London, but within a fortnight they were sent down to Wonersh as a result of the intervention of Augusta Norton who, like an evil sorceress, always appeared at critical moments to stimulate the malignant side of her brother's nature and to encourage his disregard for Caroline's wishes.

As we know from literary tradition, hell hath no fury like that of a woman torn from her children. Early in 1838 Serjeant Talfourd again introduced his infant custody legislation, and Caroline lobbied tirelessly in its support. She wrote letters to virtually all her political friends, including Edward Bulwer (later Lord Lytton), who had permitted his children to live with their mother after the failure of his marriage in 1836. Caroline was entirely familiar with Bulwer's affairs , and, judging by the consideration he had shown Mrs. Bulwer, she thought he might readily be persuaded to support Talfourd's bill. During March she wrote Bulwer several letters, expounding on the particular intensity of love any woman unhappy in marriage must feel for her children, and pleading for his assistance for the sake of all women unjustly separated from their offspring:

> May I hope, from your own generosity and kindness in permitting Mrs. Bulwer to have her little ones under her care, that you are against the separation of mother and child? May I hope that from the tenor of your feelings on other . . . public topics, you are against all tyrannies, even this, which men defend as *a right*?[25]

Although Bulwer, who had come to doubt the wisdom of his own liberality in the face of his wife's wanton abuse of his concessions, neither spoke nor voted for the bill, many of Caroline's entreaties met with better results, and the Infant Custody Bill passed the Commons in May.

13

Talfourd's bill, and the reform in the social status of women it portended, occasioned great alarm in the hearts of many English males rigidly wedded to the traditional Pauline view of woman's subalternity. In July, less than a month before the bill was to be presented to the House of Lords, an article blasting both the bill and the doctrine of sexual equality appeared in John Kemble's *British and Foreign Review*.[26] The long, anonymous essay (55,000 words), actually written by Kemble himself, was obviously designed to take advantage of popular reaction against approval of Talfourd's legislation by the House of Commons and to influence the Lords against the bill while there was still time. The article gave full details of Caroline's connection with the bill and made the most malicious suggestions about her character and personal life. Kemble implied that the passage of such legislation would encourage female profligacy and signal the destruction of the family as the foundation of society. And, he argued, the sponsorship by a brazen adultress and "renowned agitatrice"[27] like Caroline Norton ought to alert the peers to the disastrous consequences of approving Talfourd's bill. It is, of course, impossible to know if Kemble's article influenced the upper house. In any case, the bill was bitterly opposed by a majority headed by Lord Brougham, and in August it was rejected.

Caroline had no means of seeking legal reparation for Kemble's attack without the cooperation of her husband. She retaliated, therefore, with a letter, published in *The Examiner* on August 26, which simply protested the charges against her character and denied that she ever challenged the doctrine of female subordination. Indeed Caroline always dissociated herself from the preachings of Mary Wollstonecraft, Harriet Martineau, and other "new women," and she repeatedly contended in print that her efforts to remedy the injustice of the law of custody should not connect her in the public mind with the ill-advised attempts of those women who demanded absolute legal equality. In February, 1839, under the pseudonym

"Pearce Stevenson," Caroline published "A Plain Letter to the Lord Chancellor on the Infant Custody Bill," renewing her indictment of a law that denied innocent women access to their own children and urging immediate passage of new legislation. Too spirited to admit defeat or to be deterred by social embarrassment, Caroline again gave lively dinner parties, and she went out constantly, always campaigning for the new Infant Custody Bill, which was reintroduced that spring. In the summer the bill was at last approved by both the Commons and the Lords, and though the concessions made were slight, the first blow for recognition of the rights of women had been struck. Harriet Martineau and other single-minded feminist reformers were skeptical of Caroline's motives and slow to acknowledge her accomplishments, but Caroline had every reason to take principal credit for the triumph of the new custody law. She was determined to have justice, and her political craft, coupled with her formidable charm and persuasiveness, as well as her sheer endurance, resulted in a personal victory that benefited her entire sex.

In spite of the new legislation, however, Norton for some time still refused to grant his wife access to their children, and, when Caroline applied for legal intervention, she discovered that the children's domicile in Scotland put them beyond the jurisdiction of the English court. It was perhaps this final disappointment, after redress seemed so certain, that embittered Caroline most of all. Her wrongs were fast becoming an obsession with her, and she soon acquired a reputation "as a sort of professional injured person,"[28] theatrically recounting her tragic history to anyone who would listen. Despite Melbourne's attempts to control her indiscretions, both for her sake and for his, she would periodically treat the press to a recapitulation of the whole sordid history of her marriage, reminding the public of a scandal they might otherwise have forgotten. Her troubles were very real, however, and they were largely unrelieved until the spring of 1841, when the boys were sent to an English school. Even then

Norton opposed her until the death of the youngest child in the autumn of 1842 rendered him somewhat less arrogant in his treatment of Caroline and the two remaining boys. Actually Caroline was rarely troubled by Norton's hostility after 1842; she had many friends, both old and new, and she gradually climbed back from the depth of her misfortunes. "A witty woman," as Meredith wrote, "is such salt that, where she has once been tasted, she must perforce be missed more than any of the absent, the dowering heavens not having yet showered her like very plentifully upon us."[29]

Virtually all of Caroline's letters written to Melbourne from the time of the trial until the collapse of his administration in 1841 are bitter and indignant. She never tired of lacerating him for his desertion in the summer of 1836 and later for his relationships with other women and for his obstinate refusal to present her to the queen. Clearly Melbourne was partly responsible for her terrible position, and he undoubtedly deserved her indignation, though he found it convenient to ignore her allegations and to attribute her displeasure to the unreasonable passions of a "giddy, dangerous, imprudent woman."[30] After his retirement, however, Melbourne came back into Caroline's life. He frequently dined at her uncle Charles Sheridan's home in Bolton Street, and they had long leisurely conversations and sometimes went to the theater. Caroline's fury at his neglect for years after the trial had apparently subsided, and Melbourne likewise seemed to have forgiven the embarrassments occasioned by her self-advertisement and her reckless and relentless demands for his attention. During his last years Melbourne was away from London at Brocket most of the time, and Caroline's final letters were addressed to him there. Saucy and impudent as ever, she was quick to censure his indolence, to chastise him for not writing to her, and to tease him about his vain dissatisfaction with life out of office. But these letters also evidence a touching sympathy for the depression that blighted Melbourne's old age, and they were designed to cheer him and to occupy his mind.

Caroline lived for nearly thirty years after Melbourne's death,[31] visiting her sons, [32] working at her poetry or fiction, and occasionally writing pamphlets protesting the legal helplessness of English women. For a time in the mid-1840s she was often seen in the company of Lord Pembroke's son, Sidney Herbert, whom London gossips named Melbourne's successor in Caroline's most intimate affections; and two years after Norton's death in 1875, she married her old friend, Sir William Stirling-Maxwell. She was sixty-nine, he ten years younger; she died months later, he the next year.

William Melbourne, however, was the love of her life, the object of her most ardent passion. "To be pointedly rational," said Diana Warwick, "is a greater difficulty to me than a fine delirium."[33] The majority of the letters in this volume were written by a decidedly intemperate Caroline Norton, and they have the supreme value of capturing a sense of her boundless vitality at its height. From them we gain a better idea of her than from any description. She never knew when to stop, when to demur, when to exercise discretion, and in writing to Melbourne she made no attempt to veil or to moderate her feelings of love, anger, jealously, self-pity, or self-disgust.

> So well she acted all and every part
>   By turns — with that vivacious versatility,
> Which many people take for want of heart.
>   They err — 'tis merely what is called mobility,
> A thing of temperament and not of art,
>   Though seeming so, from its supposed facility;
> And false — though true; for surely they're sincerest
> Who are strongly acted on by what is nearest.[34]

It is Caroline's unbridled display of her changeable, always urgent emotions and impressions, indicating that Melbourne was something more than the dear friend hitherto assumed, that particularly justifies the publication of this work.

17

1. George Meredith, *Diana of the Crossways* (New York: Modern Library, 1931), p. 2. All subsequent references are to this edition.

Meredith's novel owed much of its popular success to its manifest depiction of the career of Caroline Norton, whose life and character are given a largely sympathetic and accurate reading. However, Diana Warwick's irresponsible revelation of a secret of national consequence implies, incorrectly, that Caroline Norton was in fact involved in the premature disclosure in December, 1845, of Sir Robert Peel's sudden determination to repeal the Corn Laws. At the time Mrs. Norton was widely accused of at least partial responsibility, but a subsequent inquiry proved the charge to be false. Meredith prefaced the 1890 and subsequent editions of *Diana of the Crossways* with the note, "A lady of distinction for wit and beauty, the daughter of an illustrious Irish house, came under the shadow of a calumny. It has lately been examined and exposed as baseless. The story of *Diana of the Crossways* is to be read as fiction."

2. Clarke Olney, "Caroline Norton to Lord Melbourne," p. 258.

3. Ibid.

4. Mabell, Countess of Airlie, *Lady Palmerston and Her Times,* 1:137–38. The three Sheridans were afterward Mrs. Norton, Helen, Lady Dufferin, and Georgiana, Lady Seymour (later duchess of Somerset).

5. Meredith, *Diana of the Crossways,* p. 3.

6. Henry Edward Fox Holland, *The Journal of the Honourable Henry Edward Fox, 1818–1830,* ed. the Earl of Ilchester, p. 272. According to one of these stories, when a certain John Talbot, who had met Caroline but once, addressed her at a gathering of London élite, she exclaimed: "Jack, Jack, for shame! We must not be too familiar in public." On another occasion, not long after her marriage, Caroline informed her husband, before a roomful of people at Chesterfield House, that she had once been madly in love with Lord Chesterfield and that he still carried her picture near his heart. In truth, she scarcely knew Chesterfield at all. In her biography Jane Gray Perkins records another Caroline Norton story, of somewhat similar import, involving Thomas Moore: One evening when Moore and Caroline were walking together, Moore happened to mention that he did most of his writing in his garden or his fields. "One would guess that of your poetry," Caroline responded. "It quite smells of them" (Jane Grey Perkins, *The Life of the Honourable Mrs. Norton,* p. 46). Apparently Moore appreciated Caroline's audacious wit. He was always her devoted friend, and in 1831 dedicated to her his poem "Summer Fête."

7. Edward L. Pierce, *Memoir and Letters of Charles Sumner,* 2:62.

8. Caroline Norton's assets survived both time and a disastrous marriage. In 1847, Thackeray credited her with "Sheridan's genius and sweet Cecilia's eyes and voice." In the following year he wrote to Lady Castlereagh of a visit to the duke of Devonshire in the company of Mrs. Norton, "she sitting bodkin in her own brougham, and indeed there are very few more beautiful bodkins in the world" (William Makepeace Thackeray, *The Letters and Private Papers of*

William Makepeace Thackeray, ed. Gordon N. Ray, 2:264, 373). Also in 1848, Jane Welsh Carlyle described her as "a beautiful witty graceful woman — whatever else" (Jane Welsh Carlyle, *Jane Welsh Carlyle: Letters to Her Family, 1839–1863,* ed. Leonard Huxley, p. 309).

9. Olney, "Caroline Norton to Lord Melbourne," p. 256.

10. Melbourne made the acquaintance of Lord Branden, an Irish peer in holy orders, and his wife during his 1827–28 tour of duty as chief secretary for Ireland. While in Dublin, Melbourne was the constant companion of Lady Branden, who lived apart from her husband, and when he returned to London in 1829, she followed. Lord Branden subsequently brought suit for damages against Melbourne in a criminal conversation action, but the case was non-suited for lack of evidence.

11. George Gordon, Lord Byron, *Don Juan* (XIV, xli).

12. See Olney, "Caroline Norton to Lord Melbourne," p. 258.

13. It was at the Nortons' home in 1831 that Benjamin Disraeli, at the time an unsuccessful candidate for a parliamentary seat, met Melbourne and confided to him his intention of one day being prime minister, a consummation that the home secretary assured him was most unlikely.

14. After Sir Robert Peel's resignation in April, 1835, there was talk of Melbourne's forming with Peel a moderate Whig-Tory coalition. Melbourne proposed that Lord Brougham, the chancellor in his first administration, be sacrificed for Lord Lyndhurst, and Lyndhurst was sounded on the proposal by Disraeli, through the agency of Mrs. Norton and at the direct instigation of Melbourne. The plan proved unsuccessful, but Caroline Norton made a lasting enemy of Brougham, who later revenged himself by opposing the Infant Custody Bill she sponsored. Undoubtedly Brougham was especially resentful of Caroline's part in the plan for his exclusion, since he had once been enamored of her and had given her every indication of his high regard when they were both in Paris during the autumn of 1834.

15. David Cecil, *Lord M.: Or the Later Life of Lord Melbourne,* p. 152.

16. Caroline was a prime target for unscrupulous journalists such as William Maginn, who boasted that during the spring of 1836 he wrote simultaneously in papers of opposing political bias two contradictory accounts of the Norton-Melbourne case. One of his stories "vilified Mrs. Norton as a debauched and profligate adventuress, while the other declared her purity with exaggerated moral fervour" (Michael Sadleir, *Bulwer: A Panorama: Edward and Rosina, 1803–1836,* p. 246 n).

17. Olney, "Caroline Norton to Lord Melbourne," p. 255.

18. Alice Acland, *Caroline Norton,* p. 55; Cecil, *Lord M.,* pp. 71–72. Also see Bertram Newman, *Lord Melbourne,* p. 213 ff; William M. Torrens, *Viscount Melbourne,* pp. 408–11; and Perkins, *Mrs. Norton,* pp. 94–95.

19. Olney, "Caroline Norton to Lord Melbourne," p. 259.

20. Ibid.

19

21. Airlie, *Lady Palmerston*, 1:190.

22. Charles Brookfield and Frances Brookfield, *Mrs. Brookfield and Her Circle*, 1:210. The letter from William Brookfield to Mrs. Jane Brookfield was written on March 26, 1847.

23. The duchess of Sutherland, later Queen Victoria's mistress of the robes and her most beloved friend, was always one of Caroline Norton's most loyal and influential supporters. Nonetheless, even the duchess once commented, in reference to Caroline's notorious impropriety, "She is so nice, what a pity she is not *quite* nice; for if she were quite nice she would be so *very* nice" (Brookfield and Brookfield, *Mrs. Brookfield and Her Circle*, 2:525). Caroline dedicated her 1839 *The Dream, and Other Poems,* probably her best volume of verse, to the duchess.

24. Acland, *Caroline Norton*, p. 107.

25. Victor Bulwer, Earl of Lytton, *The Life of Edward Bulwer, First Lord Lytton*, 1:517. When Caroline realized that her letters to Bulwer were a blunder, she hastened to write a note of apology for any pain or embarrassment she might have caused him (see Acland, *Caroline Norton*, pp. 121–22).

26. [John Kemble], "Custody of Infants Bill," pp. 269–411.

27. John Killham suggests in his *Tennyson and ThePrincess* (pp. 142–76) that Kemble's description of Caroline Norton may have influenced Tennyson's modeling of the militant heroine of *The Princess*, which he began in 1839. Like Mrs. Norton, whom Kemble termed the "bold Brandamante of the nineteenth century," Tennyson's princess is a conscious rebel who believes her sex unjustly used and does battle with male society. It is finally the war between the sexes, however, more than the princess, that Tennyson burlesques. Tennyson first met Caroline on January 26, 1845, at a dinner party given by Samuel Rogers, and he was not favorably impressed. Henry Crabb Robinson wrote of the poet's description of the event, "Tennyson did not hesitate to say that he shuddered sitting by her side, a strange remark from a young man" (Henry Crabb Robinson, *Henry Crabb Robinson on Books and Their Writers*, ed. Edith J. Morley, 2:650).

28. Cecil, *Lord M.*, p. 305. Caroline Norton's exhibitionist egotism and her habitual theatricality aroused the disapproval of a number of her contemporaries. Harriet, Lady Granville, who never forgave Caroline for an idle flirtation with her brother, the duke of Devonshire, viewed her ploys for male attention with particular repugnance. Addressing her sister, Lady Morpeth, in 1831, Lady Granville wrote about an anticipated visit from Mrs. Norton: "I am sorry we are to have an original among us, somebody impossible to like and ungracious to dislike. I am happy to think that Craddock and Walewski are to be with us; a great relief to the sober part of the community, to have such game for her to point at" (Acland, *Caroline Norton*, p. 51). Six years later Fanny Allen described a similar uneasiness about Caroline's company in a letter to her niece, Elizabeth Wedgwood: "Mrs. Norton is a fine actress, scarcely inferior to Grisi, I think. . . . Everything she does or says is so perfectly

sensible and in good taste, and yet I should say she is not attractive" (Henrietta Litchfield, ed., *Emma Darwin: A Century of Family Letters,* 1:283). And in 1854, Elizabeth, Lady Eastlake, the noted essayist and wife of Sir Charles Lock Eastlake, met Caroline in Venice and subsequently wrote about her: "No one can compare with her in telling a story — so pointed, so happy, and so easy; but she is rather a professed story teller, and brings them both in and out of season, and generally egotistically. . . . No, she is a perpetual actress, consummately studying and playing her part, and that always the attempt to fascinate — she cares not whom" (Acland, *Caroline Norton,* pp. 208–9).

29. Meredith, *Diana of the Crossways,* p. 173.

30. Quoted by Cecil, *Lord M.,* p. 309.

31. At his death Melbourne left a letter for his brother Frederick in which he made financial bequests to both Caroline Norton and Lady Branden.

32. Fletcher Norton died of consumption in Paris in 1859. Brinsley, who survived his mother by only a few months, died in Italy in 1877.

33. Meredith, *Diana of the Crossways,* p. 10.

34. Byron, *Don Juan* (XVI, xcvii). Byron defined "mobility" as "an excessive susceptibility of immediate impressions — at the same time without *losing* the past; and [it] is, though sometimes apparently useful to the possessor, a most painful and unhappy attribute."

The Letters

1

Dearest Lord,

I am very dull — how are you? Allow me to give you a
description of the way in which we pass our days. Established in
what the innkeepers call two "cheerful rooms" (looking due
east), the sun wakes us all at six. We turn our backs upon it and
lie till nine, at which time we open our dazzled eyes & dress. We
eat our breakfast in solemn silence as is meet & fit in the hall of
Seymour's ancestors. After this repast, we two females do a little
needlework, while Seymour reads Mackintosh.[2] Many times do
we inspect our watches, and sometimes order the cook in our
despair to produce dinner at a moment's notice! at *three* is our
general hour, and I feel a moment's revived energy when cherry
tart appears on the festal board. I am also amused by the act of
drinking perry.[3]

　　After dinner Georgia's sopha is wheeled out on the green,
together with a large arm chair & table for me, & a dumb waiter
for the wine and biscuits. The pet lamb is tied to a stone urn in
the centre; the parrot is put in the sun; and a beagle puppy which
had the good luck to be trod on in early infancy and therefore
made a pet of, is laid down on the grass between us. Sometimes
Seymour sits with us & is with difficulty prevailed on to rise and
help us to what fruit there may be (usually little black cherries)
but in his more industrious moments he takes a gun and shoots a
young rabbit for the gamekeeper to bait his traps with. *I* write, as
much as I can, & the intervals are filled up by Georgia's calls to
me for assistance in the management of the menagerie. The

parrot takes a shivering fit, the lamb entangles *all* its feet in the cord intended merely to tether it, and the puppy eats a cambric pocket handkerchief a day. Today my feelings so far got the better of me that I said I wished the one pet *roasted* and the other *hanged* — which set Seymour into one of his father's laughs and occupied us till tea-time. After tea I am allowed a quiet hour while the young couple caress one another. This, as I am of a social turn of mind, is quite as dull to *me* as any of the foregoing occupations of the day: and at nine o'clock, (or *ten* at the latest) I am obliged *willy nilly* to "retire to rest!" as Georgia says it *fidgets* her to know that Seymour and I are sitting down stairs after she is in bed! He makes a stout fight however & sits up till 12 and I follow his example (when safely lodged in my own room) and remain till 2 or 3 in the morning yawning & scribbling.

It is two now, so good night, and recommending the "day at Bradley" as a model for Brocket Hall.

Believe me ever
Yours very truly
Caroline Norton

1. Maiden Bradley was the Wiltshire country seat of Lord Seymour (1804–55), heir to the eleventh duke of Somerset, who in 1830 married Caroline Norton's younger sister Georgiana. Though perhaps not quite so clever as Caroline, Lady Seymour was accomplished in her own right, and she was regarded as one of the preeminent beauties in England. Caroline passed virtually the entire summer of 1831 at Maiden Bradley.

2. James Mackintosh (1765–1832) was a noted proponent of liberal Whig reform and the author of *Vindiciae Gallicae* (1791) and the posthumously .published *History of the Revolution in England* (1834).

3. A fermented drink made from the juice of pears.

2

My love for the purity of English composition compels me to remark that to the best of my belief *despatch* signifies the thing sent, and *dispatch* the hurry with which it was sent off. (*or vice versa.*) Send me Taylor's[1] letter to you — I was charmed with his complaint that he might not see his [torn] beloved except at 3 yards distance & under the surveillance of a watchman.

Write to me and tell me about yourself & public affairs.

Yrs C.

1. Probably Henry Taylor (1800–1886; knighted 1869), who proved to be a dear friend and advocate of Caroline's after her separation from Norton. (See Perkins, *Mrs. Norton,* pp. 156–57 for Mrs. Norton's October, 1839, congratulatory letter to Taylor on the ocassion of his marriage to Theodosia Alice Spring-Rice.)

℥

Maiden Bradley. August 1/31

My dear Lord

You were so agitated in your attempt to contradict my suspicions & soothe my fury respecting the fair maid of Windsor, that you actually franked your epistle back *in June!* So that even your august signature was of no avail, and Georgia and I both laughed. The scandal I hinted at, respecting H. Mys Chamberlain[1] came from two different sources; *both* tellers being very nearly related to Will 4 and neither of them being aware of the generous confidence placed in me by the other. Therefore at least most loyal & incensed nobleman acquit me of *inventing it.* If you had but lived in Prince Charlie's time, you might have acquired great honors by your immaculate devotion to the "constituted authorities" of the day.

For a more serious sentence on Susan's[2] destiny, the school I wish you to place her at, is not at Guildford but at "the Vicarage, Kingston," which is about *eleven* miles from the metropolis, and consequently nearer than Brentwood by more than one third of the distance. Your next question puzzles me: "is it not possible to put her *now*, in a way of getting her own living." Certainly it is possible, but in no mode that would continue to her the rank of gentlewoman, which in spite of the bar sinister, I understood she was to enjoy. She is 13 is she not? At 13 you may apprentice her to a staymaker, dressmaker, or some such employment but *only* in this way can you provide that she should begin at such an early age to earn her own bread. *A governess* is the only profession you can give her, which would at once secure her an income from her own exertions, and continue her among her own sex as "*a lady.*" She would also in that case have a respectable home & protection, which I do not see how she is other wise to obtain. The salaries given to governesses are large, and she would be well recommended. In this case you would still be obliged to continue her at school for two years or more, to enable her to teach others. My Miss Taylor was a governess herself previous to setting up a school, and lived a great many years in one family, the youngest of whom was afterwards sent to the school, which proved at least that the mother was satisfied with the care *five* girls (all now married) had received from Miss T. I think £60 was the sum stipulated for the education of Susan as a *boarder* at the Vicarage, but if you fixed upon her being a governess, she could go as a *half-boarder,* which is the way in which all governesses begin, and she is immediately initiated into the art of teaching, while at the same time she is taught the same as the *boarders*. It is also considerably cheaper, in consideration of the assistance supposed to be rendered to the schoolmistress by the juvenile beginner; I believe a premium is paid as with an apprentice, & then no more.

And now that I have laboured thro' this dry explanation, allow me to remark that I perceive things in your letter "which neither my character, nor my feelings, nor my situation will permit me to pass over without rebuke."

Seriously to speak, I think you are weary of this self imposed burden of a little girl who must be fed, clothed, & grow into a woman. When you weakly allowed her to be domesticated as *a plaything* in your house, you consulted your own caprice or that of Lady Caroline, and not the good of the child. When after the death of her protectress you sent her to be educated as a gentlewoman instead of *then* placing her with some respectable person as an apprentice, you again consulted only the impulse of temporary feeling, for you told me yourself that one of your reasons for so dealing by her was "that she was accustomed to have every thing the same as Caroline & to go out with her in the carriage.[''] You are now endeavouring among all the irresolute *half-decisions* which fill your august mind, to fix upon one which will meet the approval of Lady Bessboro's[3] maid, and put bread into Susan's mouth. You are annoyed and surprised & finding that you must provide for a future in which you have no personal interest, merely because in a rash moment you let a little thing in a coral necklace & sash run about your drawing room years ago. . . . You have done a good and generous action *if* it is persisted in; you have indulged a selfish and childish caprice, if you are now wearily turning over in your mind, in what way you can rid yourself of a tiresome responsibility. Send her to some good school as a half-boarder — let her be educated & recommended as a governess — and I will promise never to lose sight of her. If I have daughters she might be with me if she liked it hereafter — at any rate it is the most feasible plan, the only decent termination to what you have already done for her. *Make up your mind, at all events.* It is not surely so very difficult to decide on what you are able & willing to do in a case which must have occasionally presented itself to you for some years. If there is any thing which seems harsh to you in all I have said you will forgive it. The situation in life of this child is nothing to me except as far as it regards you, and I have often told you, and have repeated now, not *my wish* on the subject but what I think *you ought to do.*

I am still enamoured of Caleb Williams.[4] It is one of my manias that the English law does *not* protect the lower orders against the higher. Who was it answered someone who affirmed the laws were open to the poor as well as the rich, *"So is the St James's coffee house"*. Did you go to Chevening?[5] I admire your say[ing] one should not be conceited, and then talking of your eyebrows in rivalry with mine. Fie! yours were only made to shadow your eyes that mine might not dazzle you too much. Frank's[6] amours are I think come to an end, as he says the extreme forwardness of the lady "caused him to take up the bucket of weariness, filled with the waters of disgust, & dash it over his ardor." Farewell dearest Lord; dont be angry with me for my impatience on the subject of your protegée; let me think as romantically of your proceedings as I can, and believe me with more truth than many who never trouble themselves to say more than flattering words to you,

Yrs Ever
Caroline Norton

1. Perhaps William John Scott, ninth baron Napier (1786–1834), who distinguished himself at the Battle of Trafalgar and served as lord of the bedchamber to William IV from 1830 until 1833, when he was appointed special trade commissioner at Canton, China. I have only intuition, however, to support this conjectural identification.

2. A child whom Lady Caroline Lamb in one of her moments of sentimental benevolence had included in her ménage. William Lamb, usually indulgent of her whims, had agreed to the arrangement, and now, three and a half years after his wife's death, he found himself confronted with the problem of providing for Susan's future.

3. Lady Bessborough (d. 1821) was the mother of Caroline Lamb and the wife of Frederick Brabazon (Ponsonby), third earl of Bessborough (1758–1844). Caroline's grandfather, Richard Brinsley Sheridan, was for many years consumed with a great passion for Lady Bessborough, and he vowed on his deathbed that his eyes would be fixed on her for eternity.

4. William Godwin's crime and revenge novel (1794), remembered primarily for its attack on social privilege.

5. Located near Westerham, Chevening, the seat of Philip Henry Stanhope, fourth earl (1781–1855), was built circa 1630 and is one of the many houses ascribed to Inigo Jones, although there is no solid evidence that he designed it.

6. A younger brother of Caroline's, Frank Sheridan died of consumption at Mauritius in 1843.

4

Dearest Lord,

Your letter, tho' franked the second of August I only got today, and my heart misgave me that my epistle had not met with the indulgence I half-hoped for it: perhaps it is the feeling of inequality between us, more than the way in which you receive my tirades, which makes me always feel as soon as my letter is in the postman's hand as if it was crammed with impertinences; wherefor yesterday I eloquently addressed my self thus: "Ass that thou art! why write two pages of disagreable [*sic*] import, for the sake of a child you never saw & whose destiny you cannot alter?" to which myself being humbled, merely replied with a sigh. Yet *some* of what I said was true, was it not? & if I mistake you sometimes, I do at least implicitly believe your contradictions.

I admire Lady Clanricarde's[1] reply beyond measure — the dignity without the vanity of woman was in it and except that I have said enough to offend, I could have wished to have said it myself. You are very apt to think current coin an excellent substitute for other treasures, I remember your saying something of the kind to me in one of our early interviews and putting me into a concealed fury.

I am glad you were amused going down the river;[2] Vernon[3] told me he saw you, and had worked himself into a perfect fume, on the imaginary point of my willingness to go in *his* barge or *your* barge! Really gentlemen should avoid all unnecessary debates during the pending of the reform bill,[4] and allow visionary difficulties to sleep in obscure forgetfulness.

Did I tell you we had sheared the lamb so as to resemble a French poodle? I have laughed ever since.

4th August /31

Dearest Lord,

— Your letter, tho' franked the second february I only got to day. and my heart misgave me that my epistle had not met with the indulgence I half-hoped for it: perhaps it is the feeling of inequality between us, more than the way in which you receive my tirades, which makes me always feel as soon as my letter is in the postman's hand as if it was crammed with impertinences; wherefore yesterday I eloquently addressed myself thus: "Ass that thou art! why write two pages of disagreeable import, for the sake of a child you never saw & whose destiny you cannot alter?" to which myself being humbler, merely replied with a sigh. Yet some of what I said was true, was it not? & if I mistake you sometimes, I do at least implicitly believe your contradictions. —

DOWNS JONES LIBRARY
HUSTON - TILLOTSON COLLEGE

I admire Lady Clanricarde's reply beyond measure _ the dignity without the vanity of woman was in it and except that I have said enough to offend, I could have wished to have said it myself. You are very apt to think current coin an excellent substitute for other treasures, I remember your saying something of the kind to me in one of our early interviews and putting me into a conceited fury.

I am glad you were amused going down the river; Vernon told me he saw you, and had worked himself into a perfect fume, on the imaginary point of my willingness to go in his barge or your barge! Really gentlemen should avoid all unnecessary debates during the pending of the reform bill, and allow visionary difficulties to sleep in obscure forgetfulness.

Did I tell you we had sheared the lamb so as to resemble a French poodle? I have laughed ever since.

My noble brother in law, Grantley, has distinguished himself by one of the very shabbiest proceedings I ever heard of.

Sir

~~Eight~~ years ago, when Norton was a young batchelor in the Temple, and the D. g. was just dead Norton had a beautiful mare which being careless-ly hunted, ran a thorn into her foot and be-came incurably lame. People sighed, lamented, swore; and agreed that as a brood mare she would be invaluable. Norton, not being able to keep mares in foal, in his Chambers at the Temple, gave the creature to Grantley with the foal ~~she has~~ then at her foot! reserving for himself the colt she was next with foal of, who was to be bred at Grantley' cost; the mare & first foal being supposed ample indemnifi'-cation. The colt turned out exceeding well; and Norton presented it to me the day before we were married - it was then rising two years old consequently useless to me, and at Grantley in Yorkshire it was suffered to remain to save expence; Grantley & his grooms occasionally talking of it as mine & telling me news of it. Last spring I asked Grantley about it and he said it was not fit to carry me

yet. _This_ spring the groom confessed to Norton
that Grantley had _sold_ the colt for 60 guineas!
I did not believe it at first, but it turns out
to be true, with this exquisite addition that
he bribed his groom to tell Norton that his
colt had been shot, and that this one which he had
sold was a different animal! The groom had
lived in the family for many years & knew
them from boys; he pointblank refused the
bribe & the lie, & there has been nothing but
swearing, quarrelling, discoveries, & lie after
lie in the nobleman's house. Norton was
highly offended, which is unusual with him
& the head of the family; & Grantley actualy
went to coax him into quietness by offering
him 11 couple of hounds; & a present he knew
Norton was anxious to give Seymour. but his
hounds were refused, & I remain inconsolable
for the loss of my bay colt with black legs.
Pity my sufferings and believe me ever
                              Yrs truly C. E. Norton.

I shall provide myself with a horse to ride
by you next year, in spite of this misfortune.

My noble brother in law, Grantley, has distinguished himself by one of the *very* shabbiest proceedings I eve[r] heard of. Six years ago, when Norton was a young batchelor [*sic*] in the Temple,[5] and old Ld. G. was just dead Norton had a beautiful mare which being carelessly hunted, run a thorn into her foot and became incurably lame. People sighed, lamented, swore, and agreed that as a brood mare she would be invaluable. Norton, not being able to keep mares in foal, in his Chambers at the Temple, *gave* the creature to Grantley with the foal then *"at her foot"* reserving for himself the colt she was next with foal of, who was to be bred at Grantley's cost, the mare & first foal being supposed ample indemnification. The colt turned out exceeding well, and Norton presented it to me the day before we were married. It was then rising two years old consequently useless to me, and at Grantley['s] in Yorkshire[6] it was suffered to remain to save expence, Grantley & his grooms occasionally talking of it as mine & telling me news of it. Last spring I asked Grantley about it and he said it was not fit to carry me yet. *This* spring the groom confessed to Norton that Grantley had *sold* the colt for 60 guineas! I did not believe it at first, but it turns out to be true, with this exquisite addition that he bribed his groom to tell Norton that *his* colt had been shot, and that this one which he had sold was a different animal! The groom had lived in the family for many years & knew them from boys; he pointblank refused the bribe & the lie, & there has been nothing but swearing, quarrelling, discoveries, & lie after lie in the nobleman's house. Norton was highly offended, which is unusual with him to the head of the family; and Grantley actualy [*sic*] went *to coax him into quietness* by offering him a couple of hounds, a present he knew Norton was anxious to give Seymour: but his hounds were refused, & I remain inconsolable for the loss of my bay colt with black legs. Pity my sufferings and believe me ever

Yrs truly,
C. S. Norton.

I shall provide myself with a horse to ride by you next year, in spite of this misfortune.

1. Harriet Canning (1804–76), only daughter of George Canning, sister of Charles John Canning, married Ulick John De Burgh (1802–74), who was created Marquess of Clanricarde in 1825 and Baron Somerhill in 1826. I am unable to identify Lady Clanricarde's "reply."

2. William IV officially opened the new London Bridge on August 1, 1831. En route to the ceremony the royal procession of some thirty boats departed from Waterloo Bridge, with Melbourne, the other cabinet ministers, and Earl Grey in the fourteenth boat, just ahead of the royal barge.

3. Possibly Granville Harcourt Vernon (1785–1861), M.P. for Lichfield from 1806 until 1831 and for Oxfordshire from 1831 until his death.

4. The second Reform Bill introduced by Earl Grey's government passed the Commons in the late summer of 1831 but was rejected by the Lords in October. The following spring, when William IV proposed the creation of fifty new peers in order to pass the act, the Tories withdrew their opposition, and the Reform Bill became law.

5. George Norton was admitted to the Middle Temple on August 14, 1820, and he was subsequently called to the English bar on November 25, 1825.

6. In addition to Wonersh Park, Grantley owned a Yorkshire estate.

5

Maiden Bradley
August 7/31

Dearest Lord

I laughed for an hour at your conduct on the occasion of Sir J. G's[1] superintendence of your accommodation, for his Majesty's memorable visit to the New bridge. You must have grown much more lusty (as the maids call it) if you thought yourself entitled to "room for two". What a pity you did not take some utterly unknown person — the bride to whom you gave the paper knife for instance — and undergone with calm philosphy the scrutiny of Sir James's glance, supported by the consciousness of innocence. I do not know what my respectable uncle might be moved to do on extraordinary occasions, but as it is, I think the only letter I ever got from him, was on the publication of The Sorrows of Rosalie[2] which began *"Beloved Sappho"* and certainly would not have reminded me that I was his niece. I think *demure* must (as that respectable authority Georgia says) come from *demur* ie. to demur at committing any impropriety. Seymour on the contrary suggests that it signifies modest retirement, from *demeurer chez soi*. I leave you to choose your own derivation.

Cant you change little Susan's name? It has been done very often in one instance under my own inspection: a little sister of Sophy Armstrong's having come to Miss Taylor's bearing the 1st Colonel's name and in consequence of certain *family arrangements* ceasing to be called Armstrong & taking instead the 2d Colonel's name, Miss *Napier!*[3] in a couple of months we had almost all forgotten the original patronymic & certainly never thought of finding any reason for the change. The situation of half boarder, as I saw it at *my* school, was not the least degrading or unpleasant. They had several little privileges which we had not, and only assisted to teach the little ones (which I did voluntarily) and had rather more embroidery & screen painting & needlework of divers kinds, which last I used to coax them into doing always for me. A *story* of the hardships of *any* situation may be made, and perhaps *one instance* given in real life; but it is to the generality of such cases we are to look, and not at an individual instance. However God knows poor little thing I do not wish to persuade you into adding anything to the discomfort of her life. Only tell me what she is to be & what you will call her & I will never speak to you in the imperative mood again. I am exceedingly offended at your quotation "See a long race," and your irony on the subject of my future family. I beg leave to mention to your Lordship that the young Lady whom you so kindly promise to take for a wife, will be born early in the ensuing November.[4] . . .

I can write no more for Seymour stands with the candle in his hand insisting on the letters going.

Farewell

Yrs ever truly

C. S. Norton

1. Sir James Graham (1792–1861), the Whig statesman, was one of the Committee of Four which prepared the 1832 Reform Bill. He was appointed lord rector of the University of Glasgow in 1838 and later home secretary in Sir Robert Peel's government. In 1819 Graham married Fanny Callander, Caroline Norton's maternal aunt.

2. Caroline Norton's first book of poems, published in 1829.

3. Probably the daughter of Lieutenant-Colonel Richard Armstrong of Lincoln and later the ward of Sir William Francis Napier (1785–1860), who became colonel in 1830 and was raised to major-general in 1841.

4. Caroline Norton's second son Brinsley was born in November, 1831.

6

Maiden Bradley, August 9th [1831]

Dearest Lord

Seymour being out, I sit down to finish my observations which he so cruelly interrupted the other day, adding to it the insult that if the police were to search me at any time they would be sure to find only a pencil, paintbrush, bunch of seals, and your last letter! He grows very grand here in the country and frequently observes how much better it is for my health & spirits to be at Bradley than any where else. I must tell you a sentence in Norton's letter announcing his august arrival the following day. Seymour promised to send the carriage for him the last stage to which kindness he thus equivocally alludes. "I shall start for Frome tomorrow, & hope, by *Seymour's kind assistance* to kiss you at nine in the evening."!! I was so enchanted at this mode of conveying his gratitude to the noble Lord, that I was obliged to read the sentence aloud, much to the confusion of all parties present. How very much out of practice Norton must have grown in that batchelor [*sic*] month in town!

I am glad Leopold[1] has acted with spirit, but I fear *great chances* are all Heaven has allotted him in this world. He is more deficient than almost any one I ever saw in the courage that defies consequences. The animal courage necessary to fight is nothing in my eyes. The man who would seize a crown must see nothing *but* that vision of Royalty. If the prospect of comparative independence has not altered Leopold into a hero, he will pause & look round him before he attempts to grasp any object.

Pray my Lord is "Duncannon's fair-haired daughter"[2] to be

put in my list with Olivia Emily & Miss Eden?[3] Answer this little query. I have just got your letter of yesterday (the second frank you have misdated) and thank you very much for the offer of a bay filly to console my desolate heart. I will ask Norton when he comes in from hunting (if he has had good sport) to let me seize the opportunity and go to Brocket to make my selection. I hope he will not be farouche about it, but I shall come to Brocket in the spring at any rate. You never tell me whether you see Augustus[4] there; does he always stay at Brocket?

I think we might have done better about Grantley if we had had your advice sooner. As it is, Norton & he are scarcely on speaking terms but Grantley is gone to Scotland and we are so accustomed to his doing shabby things, that I dare say on his return, all will proceed as usual. I never go to Wonersh and have only seen Lady G. once in two years. . . .

It is reckoned good luck for an infant to cry during the ceremony of baptism so you ought to rejoice that Lady Ashley's foal[5] lifted up its voice and wept. Is it pretty? and which side of the family does it most resemble? but men never can answer these questions.

Poor Mrs. William Ashley[6] will I think scarcely live many years. She is beyond every thing worn & delicate. A reflection which rather makes me sad, seeing that I like her and think her more beautiful than almost any one I know. What had Lady Jersey[7] to do there. Is a treaty concluded in which she agrees to be godmother, on the Punic faith?

Farewell dear Lord, you asked me rather a conceited question as to how I stood affected to you by absence. My Lord absence makes no difference with *me*; your letters do because they are the pleasantest I get. Strike the balance in your own favor and endeavour to feel humble & modest on the occasion.

Who do you call upon of a morning?

Ever yrs truly
Caroline Norton

1. Leopold, prince of Saxe-Coburg, who in 1816 had for a time been betrothed to Princess Charlotte, daughter of George IV. When William IV, sixty-four and in ill health, came to the English throne in June, 1830, it seemed quite possible that he might die before his niece, the Princess Victoria, reached her majority. There were various candidates for accession to the anticipated regency, and Leopold seemed the most likely choice. The king, however, opposed Leopold, and the Regency Act of 1830 provided that in the event of Victoria's succession to the throne during her minority, the duchess of Kent should be her daughter's guardian and serve as regent. On June 4, 1831, Leopold was elected first king of the Belgians, and he was inaugurated in Brussels on July 21. Before he had been on his throne a month, William of Orange led his Dutch army against Belgium. Leopold secured French help, but he insisted upon joining arms alone with the Dutch before the arrival of the French troops. The result was catastrophic, and, but for the immediate intervention of the French, Belgium would have been overrun. Though he salvaged his crown, Leopold was profoundly discouraged by the Ten Days' War, and to the end of his days he refused to discuss its humiliations.

2. Lady Augusta Ponsonby (b.1814), second daughter of John William Brabazon (Ponsonby), fourth earl of Bessborough and Viscount Duncannon (1781–1847), one of the Reform Bill Committee of Four, and longtime governor general of Ireland. Duncannon was the brother of Lady Caroline Lamb, and thus Melbourne's brother-in-law. Lady Augusta, who was the cherished friend of such notables as the Reverend Sydney Smith, Samuel Rogers, and Thomas Moore, was first married in 1834 to William Thomas, earl of Kerry (d. 1836), eldest son of the third marquess of Lansdowne. In 1845 she married the Hon. Charles Gore, by whom she had five children.

3. Emily Eden (1797–1869), daughter of William Eden, first baron Auckland, and sister of George Eden, the second baron, who in 1835 succeeded Lord Hastings as governor general of India. The author of several books, including two popular novels, *The Semi-detached House* (1859) and *The Semi-attached Couple* (1860), Miss Eden was a prominent figure among London's social elite, and her home, Eden Lodge, in Kensington, was frequented by all the luminaries of the day. For many years she was an intimate friend of Melbourne's and presumably Caroline Norton's rival for his regard. Certainly Mrs. Norton had little affection for Emily Eden, and the feeling appears to have been mutual. In a December 15, 1833, letter to Mrs. Theresa Lister, Miss Eden wrote of an anticipated visit to Bowood, Lord Lansdowne's country estate, where she expected to encounter Caroline Norton: "I hear the Nortons are to be there, which will be funny. I do not fancy her, but still she will be amusing to meet for once." (Perhaps this meeting was the occasion of the "scene with E. Eden" that Caroline recalled in Letter 26.) Some six months thereafter, following Melbourne's selection as prime minister, Miss Eden mentioned Mrs. Norton in a letter to Lady Pamela Campbell, in which she denominated Caroline the "Fornarina," probably alluding to the famous "Fornarina" to whom Raphael dedicated his sonnets: "Lord Melbourne made a

good start in the House of Lords as far as speaking went. I do not know what ladies have hopes of him, but the 'Fornarina,' as he calls her himself, has him in greater thraldom than ever" (Emily Eden, *Miss Eden's Letters,* ed. Violet Dickinson, pp. 230, 240–41).

The "Olivia Emily" Caroline also included in her "list" of rivals was Melbourne's niece, Lady Emily Caroline Cowper (d. 1872), eldest daughter of the fifth earl Cowper and Melbourne's sister, Emily Peniston Lamb; in 1830 Lady Emily married Anthony Ashley Cooper, seventh earl of Shaftesbury (1801–85). See also Letter 45, where Lady Emily is referred to as "Minny."

4. The epileptic and mentally deficient son of Melbourne and Caroline Lamb, Augustus lived at Brocket with his father until his death in November, 1836.

5. Anthony Ashley Cooper, eighth earl of Shaftesbury (1831–86). The eighth earl was born on the 27th of June. That summer Caroline wrote the poem "On Seeing Anthony, the Eldest Child of Lord and Lady Ashley"; in 1836 she dedicated *A Voice from the Factories* to the seventh earl.

6. Mrs. William Ashley (d. 1891), born Maria Anne Ballie, was the wife of the younger brother of the seventh earl of Shaftesbury, William Ashley (1803–77).

7. Sarah, Lady Jersey (d. 1867), eldest daughter of the tenth earl of Westmorland and wife of George Child, fifth earl of Jersey (1773–1859), was recognized as one of the priestesses of nineteenth-century London fashion, and together with Lady Cowper she ruled Almack's for many years. Lady Jersey's sister, Lady Maria Fane (d. 1834), was the wife of Viscount Duncannon and the mother of Lady Augusta Ponsonby.

7

Dearest Lord

I trust you are very busy, sending succours to Leopold, as I have not heard from you this morning, and have got into a pernicious habit of expecting your letters at certain intervals and feeling disappointed when they do not come. Did you get that lovely anecdote of Norton requiring Seymour to assist him in the exploit of greeting me after his long absence? It is our best joke here.

Having enquired of the said Norton whether I might accept a filly from you, he very graciously responded that so high was his opinion of your personal merit that I might take *any*thing from you, and appealed to Seymour for his opinion, who answered with a grave caution peculiar to himself, that he "thought it would be very nice for me to have a horse to ride next spring." It was difficult to conjecture from this reply what degree of enthusiasm he possessed in common with N.[orton] on your various merits, but the latter was quite satisfied that they mutually understood each other, and agreed perfectly, wherefore, turning to me he ordered me to enquire the ages of the said fillies, and to accept the quietest, as mares were not to be trusted. I eagerly parried this attack on my courage, by reminding him that Georgia's horse was a mare (Cinderella) and had been constantly rode by me. He gradualy [*sic*] became convinced by my eloquence, and eulogised your kindness; after which he became less *"luminous* and *comprehensible"*[1] having involved himself in some abstruse internal argument on the comparative dangers to my moral character & physical strength, of rides on Carthugh's[2] kicking horse Selim, or frequent caracoles on your mare in the Park.

A man of the name of Curry, has sent to assure me he has in his possession a picture of Miss Lindley[3] [*sic*] (when Mrs. S.[heridan]) holding my father in her arms: unfinished, and painted by Humphrey's[4] for my grandfather who never had it sent home as Miss L[inley] died before it was quite completed and Humphrey becoming blind and distressed *pawned* it to a Dr. Curry, (I presume a relative of the present possessor) for 10 guineas for which sum the said A. Curry offers to give it to us. Do you think the story likely? Georgia & I wish to give it to my mother if we could be sure it really *is* my father & grandmother, but all we can learn is that Charlie Norton[5] (who I heartily wish you would ask to dinner some day) says the child is a dark pale thing, and the woman "so naked, as to be almost indecent!" If you had less to do I would have asked you to look at it as you would know whether it was at all like Miss Lindleys [*sic*] other portraits. As it is we think of buying it *on the chance* as it was pawned for so little, and would be such a treasure to our hoary headed parent. The worst of it is that these people say they have *had* it *24* years and yet never offered it till now to "the fair authoress of Rosalie";[6] and we never *heard* of such a picture. Let me know your valuable opinion on the subject, and believe me in consequence of the departure of the fleet footed postman

Rashly, hastily, & scribblingly
Yours
C. Norton

1. Possibly a corruption of a line from Wordsworth's "Apology" (*Ecclesiastical Sonnets,* II, xxvi, 14): "Than the bare axe more luminous and keen." The term "luminous," however, may well have been all around Mrs.

Norton when she wrote, particularly as it was applied to literature and to the intellectual converse of an age which so prided itself on fine wit and table talk. Richard Brinsley Sheridan purportedly used the figure in 1787 in referring to the "luminous page of Gibbon" (*Sheridaniana* [London, 1826], p. 98).

2. Unidentified.

3. Caroline Norton's grandmother, Elizabeth Ann Linley, with whom, in 1772, Richard Brinsley Sheridan eloped to France and whom he later married.

4. The studio of Ozias Humphrey (1742–1810), the miniaturist and portrait painter and the intimate friend of Blake and of George Romney.

5. Charles Francis Norton (1807–35), George Norton's younger brother; an army captain. Charles's untimely death deprived Caroline of her only hope of kindness from her husband's family. However, his widow, who in 1838 married Edmund Phipps, always remained Caroline's faithful friend.

6. *The Sorrows of Rosalie.*

B

Will of the Wisp, I have no letter from you: your name is not in the Council for the 14th inst, and I believe you are entrapped and made away with. Your observations on the verb to kiss I thoroughly disapproved of, as bordering too much on a style of conversation called *coarse*: however I will modify, soften down, alter, and diminish, all the old innocent words to which the savage vulgarity of some of your sex have accorded a double signification: only I cannot learn them by instinct and it was Norton's fault, not mine, for *he* used the verb *tout simplement*. As to the effect upon my shy & most pleasant brother-in-law, I rather love putting him out of countenance, the more especially as now we are not under the parental observation of my mistaken mother, I do not share in his shyness. And Norton has no sort of objection to Seymour's doing *"what he thinks proper"* and regularly keeps Georgia's honor instead of mine and retires at ten, or sleeps quietly on the sofa during the two hours which intervene between that time and midnight (which is my earliest hour for roosting) without once mingling in our intellectual conversation.

Is Leopold beat? There is no comfort in reading the papers, they tell so many lies, and spin out alternate skirmishes & editorial observations till I grow frantic with impatience. Surely *you must* know how all the turmoil is likely to end; for I presume amid all the humbug and trickery of ministerial management; useless letters to useless ambassadors; and conferences with plenipotentiaries who have no power at all, you do in

49

fact all see your way out, as well as the lady in distress lost in a forest on the stage knows the path which is eventually to take her behind the scenes.

I trust the worry and fagging have not made you ill again. I know it is foolish expecting that you can sit down and write nonsense to me every other day, but promise me that if you *are* ill you will send one line here, where I do not meet people at every turn ready to give me the last intelligence respecting you; some out of spite and some out of good nature; as I had when you were ill in South St. this spring.

Your observation respecting the fair haired Duncannon and the Levitical law looked suspicious: we are not under the Levitical law in that instance for certainly Uncle Graham being a widower might without scruple pounce upon Georgia if single & carry her off as his bride.[1] . . . Talking of its [Maiden Bradley's] innocence and virgin appellation, it is a fact that five women have been churched since our arrival, one of whom is the mother of enormous twins! and the strict and precise Seymour was moved by this circumstance to say that he believed all the babies in the village were the offspring of his father's housekeeper, whom he politely termed Queen bee of the hive, & who is a most respectable skeleton of 60 years & upwards; very staid and stiff; dusts the old family pictures and goes to a methodist meeting-house twice every Sunday.

Lady Westmoreland[2] [*sic*] and my mother talk of coming here together; or rather to a little romantic looking inn close to Stourhead[3] which is four miles from this. There is a delay at present owing to some quarrel which Ly. W. has got into — is it with you? It is quite true that she alone and a Mr. Pig[e?]on prophecied the charming appearance I now make; and it is also equally true that I, who have made such strides in vanity since those days, as to believe people when they profess to think me handsomer than that model of beauty the Lady Seymour; did at that time consider Lady W's partiality for my looks as one of her eccentricities; and submitted to have white turbans and greek shawls pinned round my head, with precisely the feeling with which I would humour the caprices of a little child. She was very kind to me tho', and I shall be glad to receive her congratulations in person on my sudden elevation & consequent infernal coquetry [*sic*]. Truly the change has done me little good any way. I was at least a good, honest hearted, merry little brown wench in those days, and cared little who thought me plain because I had never [known] a difference of opinion on the subject.

[Norton and Sey]mour rush about the country hunting hares with the beagle harriers. I would not have believed the latter had been so active & punctual; he fixes his hunting horn at six and is in his saddle as the clock strikes; flies about here & there & every where; and goes as mad about a fine day or a moonlight night, pheasant's egg and light rifles, as my little brother Charlie.[4] Rural intelligence is out of the question; I have not seen one human being since I came down, except the Duke's Steward or bailiff or agent or whatever the man is called.

I will bring you a little drawing or two, when I return. Meanwhile tell me what you are at & where Susan is deposited.

And believe me ever yrs truly

Caroline Norton

1. Melbourne had evidently jested in a recent letter about the impossibility of a match between himself and Duncannon's daughter Augusta, because of the Levitical proscription against incest (see Lev. 18:6–18). Actually Melbourne was related to the Ponsonby family only by marriage (see above, Letter 6, n. 2).

2. Lady Westmorland (d. 1857), born Jane Saunders, was the second wife of John Fane, tenth earl of Westmorland (1759–1841).

3. Located in the village of Stourton, Stourhead mansion was built for the Hoare family by Colen Campbell in 1720–24. The Stourhead estate, best known for its marvelous lake and pleasure-grounds, was presented to the National Trust by Sir Henry Hoare in 1947.

4. Charles Sheridan (1817–47), reputed to be the handsomest and perhaps the most charming of all the Sheridan men.

[*Maiden Bradley*] *August 21/1831*

Dearest Lord

I got your letter yesterday, when I was on the point of scribbling to you but was prevented by "being in trouble" as the maids say, about my child, who has been pining ever since he came here and has now got a swelling in the glands of his throat which looks as large as a goitre. Having however received Herbert's[1] opinion, coinciding with that of the medical man whom I have employed here, I make myself as easy as I can about him. I have not the direction of the woman who is in possession of my grandmother's picture, and only know that her name is *Curry* and her house opposite the Milbanke penitentiary:[2] but Charlie Norton has a perfect knowledge of these facts, and if you really *could* spare so much time as to look at it, your servant could enquire the direction from him at my house. It would be a great pleasure to us to have it here, when my mother comes to Stourton, which we expect will be in a week as Lady Westmoreland [*sic*] and she were to have set off yesterday for Portsmouth.[3] I read Lady W's letter to you and thought it very kind, though odd, and *like her* — but surely you must have lived among very selfish people to make a few expressions of kindness & interest seem of so much value. To me it appears as if it were impossible to think of you, or her whose talents and defects have so often been described to me, *without* interest, and that of no common kind. I am sorry for poor Lord Duncannon, remembering my own most lovely brother Tom who was killed on board Ld Napier's[4] ship at Rio Janiero [*sic*], and I have a prejudice in favor of the profession of a sailor. They are in general braver and more frank hearted than other men & (what women value) are fonder of their *homes*.

I do not think myself *enormously* vain: there is a boundary to a fault when one is conscious of it: but what you say respecting the suddenness of any desirable acquisition turning one's head, I have often pleaded when told by my friends how much vainer I was than Georgia who was twice as handsome. People whose beauty is a familiar thing to their ears from childhood, might as well be vain of it as of being able to read and write. In all events you need not fear personal vanity ruining me *now,* as I have always the pleasing reflection to recur to, that I have not, in spite of the change of opinion among my friends on the score of my looks, obtained what I wished — perhaps I should say what I *expected* when I first began to look in the glass with satisfaction.

I promise faithfully to take care of you in the general convulsion: I will keep you in a small light room adjoining mine & feed you on split peas as we do the doves. I trust in Heaven we shall neither of us see the day that will make the proposal less a jest than it seems now. I am sorry for my Prince,[5] and should think the English after grumbling at the pension they themselves bestowed on this grafted scion of British royalty would take particularly amiss the expence of a war to support his title in Belgium, and the taxes which I presume would afterward be laid on light, air, and the free use of one's limbs. I cannot comprehend his accepting Belgium after refusing Greece.[6] I say old boy if I wrote to him would Ld Palmerston[7] send it? He promised to write to *me*; but that was when he was safe in the red hall of Marlboro' House. Who will he marry when all this is over, provided it ends well for him?[8]

I had an official communication from your brother George[9] on the subject of providing for my nurse's husband. It was very kind of him to answer me so soon as he did, and struck Georgia with great admiration for him, as she loves punctuality in matters of business, and is beginning to think she too ought to have a "pet Lamb" as she very impertinently expresses herself when she speaks of you. Meanwhile I am very anxious to see this man provided for, for the nurse does nothing but weep over him and run after [him] and he is always in my house. They talk of the winter as if he was to die of the frost; and of next summer [as if] it would only shine on his corpse like a dead fly of last season. Help me if you can at any time in this matter, and I faithfully promise it shall be the *very last time*, as children who dread a whipping mendaciously assure their instructors, that I will torment you. Do not think that I am discontented with *short* letters, it is only when I am entirely left to my own conjectures that I grow anxious; it is sufficient, while I feel that you are so much occupied with graver matters, to hear that you are well and going to spend the ensuing Saturday at Brocket or Chevening, *as may be*. This I hope you will still continue to tell me.

Believe me ever truly yrs
Caroline Norton

1. Apparently the Sheridan family physician.

2. Millbank Prison, originally known as the Penitentiary, which was constructed between 1813 and 1816 and demolished in 1892–93. The Tate Gallery is now located on the site of the old Penitentiary.

3. See above, Letter 8.

4. The ninth baron Napier (see above, Letter 3, n. 1). Duncannon's second son, William Wentworth Brabazon (b. 1812), died at sea in the summer of 1831.

5. Leopold of Saxe-Coburg. See above, Letter 6, n. 1.

6. When Greece secured independence from Turkey, in February, 1830, it appeared that Greek officials would offer their vacant throne to someone connected with the English royal family. Leopold was a leading candidate, and for a time he actively sought the Greek throne. In the spring of 1830, however, the prospect of the English regency readjusted his ambitions; and, on May 21, when the kingdom was officially offered to him, he declined.

7. Henry John Temple, third viscount Palmerston (1784–1865), became foreign secretary in Lord Grey's administration in 1830, which office, except for four months during Peel's administration, he held for eleven years. In 1830 Palmerston assisted Belgium in the successful bid to gain independence from Holland, and in February, 1831, he blocked the ascension of the French duc de Nemours to the Belgian throne. On February 3, when the Belgian National Congress selected the duc de Nemours to be king, Palmerston promptly threatened France with war. The 1815 Congress of Vienna had established Belgium and Holland as a barrier against French expansion, and England had no intention of allowing a French annexation of Belgium.

8. On August 9, 1832, Leopold married Louise D'Orleans, the eldest daughter of King Louis-Philippe of France.

9. George Lamb (1784–1834), Melbourne's youngest brother, whose paternity is generally ascribed to the prince regent, later George IV. In 1809, Lamb married Caroline St. Jules, daughter of the fifth duke of Devonshire and Lady Elizabeth Foster, the duke's mistress, whom Devonshire married after the death of his duchess, Georgiana.

10

[*Maiden Bradley*] *August 25* [*1831*]

Dearest Lord

A thousand thanks for your kindness with regard to the picture, and indeed I blush to think that my innocence so misled me as to make me suppose there was but *one* penitentiary[1] in the City of Crime of which you are an inhabitant and Poodle Byng[2] Comissioner [*sic*] of Supplies. I have written to bid Chas Norton instantly purchase it from the hands of the fair widow & am very glad it has turned out a true portrait. Its faults will be of no consequence in my mother's eyes & I doubt not but that she will discover a likeness in the child to my father when she married him; so once more many thanks for Georgia & myself.

Your assertion respecting your youth is curious: When *I* was whipped in days of yore, I always defied consequences, bit the fingers of the whipper in, and rushed to repeat my crime, — which proves that it was good for you to be whipped and very bad for me. I can recollect no single instance in which I was subdued by harshness and I think it is a general mistake, governing children by "force of arms" which restrains the weakest only till their strength & yours are nearly on a par. My boy[3] is a little better, but he is a very sickly child, and has been so since he was six months old when Norton drove us down on a Xmas visit to Hampton Ct[4] in an open gig. The child got an inflammation on its lungs and was given over by all the medical men who saw it in consequence of this journey. Till that time it was so very pretty with its dark eyes and red cheeks, that the villagers at Long Ditton[5] called it "*Mossrose*", seeing that its

56

rosy face was surmounted by a green velvet cap of my manufacturing. Mothers always grow fonder I believe of their offspring, in proportion as they are sickly, plain, & unengaging to strangers. I scarcely cared *then* to have it with me for above an hour or two in the day, when everybody admired and begged for it as a plaything, but now that they never notice it, except to ask *what ails the creature*, I cant bear it out of my sight and think every thing it says a miracle. But enough on so small a subject. What you say of the affection subsisting between members of a large family is I think perfectly true; and the one that is gone, always *seems* the favourite of all. Faults are so soon forgotten when they have ceased to irritate us; and words and looks, that were indifferent to us while they were familiar things, seem lost treasures when they are remembered. The very empty place which we were accustomed to see always occupied by the same form, brings more bitterly home the reflection "they are all there but him —" *all* — why should *he* be taken from amongst his companions. I think it is almost worse than losing an only child, for then the mother may sit down silently in her sorrow, while in the other case she is constantly listening to the laughter & voices of her remaining children, and missing the *one* laugh & the *one* voice which she alone remembers to have mingled in the confused sounds of merriment. It keeps one's sorrow alive, which is a thing Seymour particularly objects to, and is constantly lecturing about as if it were a sin to lament more than one week for *any* relation. — The post is just gone so I must fold & seal.

Ever yrs truly
C. Norton

---

1. See above, Letter 9.

2. Sir John Byng (1772–1860), who was created Baron Stafford of Harmondsworth by Melbourne in 1835. Byng served as commander-in-chief of

the forces in Ireland in 1828, and he was appointed governor of Londonderry and Culmore in 1832. He was one of the few distinguished officers who supported Melbourne and the Whigs in their struggle to pass the 1832 Reform Bill.

3. Caroline's first son, Fletcher Spencer Norton.

4. When Thomas Sheridan died in 1816, Caroline's mother was given private apartments at Hampton Court, through the influence of the duke of York, the old friend and patron of Richard Brinsley Sheridan. Mrs. Sheridan lived at Hampton Court until her death in 1851.

5. Located a few miles west of London, in Surrey.

11

Maiden Bradley
August 26 [*1831*]

I was cruelly interrupted yesterday by Mr. Fleetfoot, the aged
Postman, when on the point of replying to that part of your
august epistle which relates to my regretting *that I had not done
as well as I might have done.* "My good man" (as my mother
say[s] to her sons-in-law when she is *very* angry) I would not
give a fillip to be a Duke's wife tomorrow. If it was mere position
in the world which I had desired, and in which I had been
disappointed, depend upon it I should not have expressed it to
you; as I *should* be ashamed of that feeling, tho not of my vanity
so much as you could wish. I am amply content to be *Mistress*
N, even without the *Honble* and have even a pleasure in feeling
when I am in company with your proud ones, that little as I am, I
am as satisfied as the best of them, perhaps more so — that I
wish for nobody's place or lot in preference to my own, and
know that they can take nothing from me, or humble me in any
one way. At least I have never been humbled *yet.*

My regret for past disappointments is of a different nature,
and happily does not prevent my having a very tolerable share of
interest in the present & future; a life is not wrecked at twenty; it
is venerable persons like yourself, who look back most bitterly
at lost opportunities & talents misused — we get over it. The
only misfortune I ever particularly dreaded, was living & dying a
lonely old maid, which I am happy to say has been prevented. I
am a *first object* with *one* person (Mr. Norton,) and a secondary
object with a good many — more, I do not desire. An old maid is

never any one's first object, therefore I object to that situation. I like to be coaxed and petted & made much of, to whip my children & give them doses of rhubarb[1] and to correspond with noblemen who direct to me Mrs. Norton. My Lord, I am contented. I have not The Faerie Queene with me, but as it is a favourite of mine I will look into it the first thing on my return, while my maid is unpacking my trunk. Many remarks *have* been made upon our acquaintance, but never one (*in my hearing*) of the satisfactory nature you suppose — nevertheless I am quite willing to believe that I am wonderfully benefitted by it, and at any rate as it is a great pleasure to me, I can the better bear doubt on the subject from "my friends and the public." Your remarks on the dangers incurred by Sir R. Adair,[2] were I presume intended to teach me refinement on my Grandfather's play.[3] eh? old boy? — Defend yourself with that mixture of mendacious eloquence and assurance which is so striking a feature of your mind.

27th

I have just received the agreeable intimation (are there two *e's* in agreeable? Seymour says there are.) that our house has become so tempting that yesterday morning between one & three *A.M.*, it was broken into, and our small stock of plate stolen therefrom; together with a silver & ebony snuff box of Nortons; a bunch of seals of different sizes with crest & arms of our illustrious ancestors etc a small parcel containing a merino dress for my little child, which I have been dying to have, as the weather is so uncertain here and he suffers so from cold, and a silver teapot belonging to the late respectable & long lamented Ld. Grantley.[4] I could not help being a little amused after the pains we took with our outside, to have our inside so cruelly plundered, and as we believe by the very man who did all our improvements, and who we now hear is the greatest rascal unhung; was refused as a policeman, on account of his bad character, and has been before the magistrate on suspicion of theft, more than once. Norton is greatly consterned [*sic*], and is now sitting with folded arms wondering what is to be done, while I, as soon as I have finished talking to you, mean to write to the active Tom Walker[5] and beseach [*sic*] his assistance to revenge the theft of my baby's blue [dress] which is the part of the burglary [illegible] *au coeur* (or in vulgar English *sticks in the gizzard*.) Charles Norton has taken every step which was necessary and if we recover any of our spoons, we shall of course be obliged to melt them into a plate or medal to present to him for a token of gratitude. Good bye. God bless you.

Yrs ever truly
Caroline Norton

28th

I have just got yr *long epistle* of this morning. I am alarmed at your taking a respectable male companion to Brocket. It looks as if you wanted to fit up yr house for a respectable female one. *Dont be extravagant.* I dare say it will hold everybody as comfortably as possible & suit the lady's maid up stairs.

1. The medicinal rhubarb (*rhubarb officinale* or *rhubarb palmatum*), used as a cathartic or tonic.

2. Sir Robert Adair (1763–1855), the diplomat and M.P. for the Whig boroughs of Appleby and Camelford and a long-time friend of Charles James Fox.

3. Presumably *The School for Scandal* (1777).

4. George Norton's uncle, William Norton, second baron Grantley (1741[2]–1822).

5. Probably the local postman. In nineteenth-century parlance the colloquial name "Tom Walker" was sometimes applied to postmen, much as "Tom Tyler" designated any common fellow, or "Tom Tug" titled a fool.

WHATEVER CORRESPONDENCE Caroline Norton may have had with Melbourne during the next four and a half years has apparently not been preserved. Probably there was little occasion for letter writing since, during most of that period, they saw each other daily, either in Storey's Gate, at Melbourne's house in South Street, Mayfair, or at his official lodgings in Downing Street. After Melbourne became prime minister in the spring of 1834, he had somewhat less time for Caroline. But the hours spent in her company, away from the vexing responsibilities and harassments of his office, were then all the more precious to him. Melbourne's position during his second ministry could hardly have been more difficult. King William and the House of Lords opposed his attempts at initiating positive legislation, and his own party constantly complained of his conservatism and his procrastination in pushing through Whig reforms. With Caroline he was able to forget his political troubles and to shake off the sad sense of alienation that haunted his later years.

Caroline left her husband for the second time in March of 1836. He, in turn, took the children away from her — which he had the legal right to do. By early April, Norton had decided on a divorce, and, emboldened by Lord Wynford, among others, he had nerved himself to bring the burgeoning scandal out into the open. His intention was commonly known in advance of his action; and, of course, gossip regarding the prime minister and Mrs. Norton had long been rife in London society, partly as a consequence of the particular attention paid their friendship by the sensational press.

When Caroline first left Norton's house in the summer of 1835, Melbourne strongly advised her to make some sort of peace with her husband and to avoid an open and final break. After the second separation Melbourne again implored her to return to Norton, lest he carry out his rumoured intentions. Perhaps more acutely than Caroline herself, Melbourne realized what she would suffer should Norton file for divorce, but his advice to her was not uninfluenced by personal concern. Though he had consistently shown a marked disregard for convention in his relationship with Caroline, Melbourne feared above everything the humiliation of a vulgar public inspection of his private life. Considering the notoriety occasioned by his difficulties with his late wife and the public awareness of *l'affaire* Branden, he was understandably anxious to avoid a new domestic scandal.

He wrote to Caroline on April 10, pleading with her to calm herself and to pursue the sensible course of reconciliation:

> I have always told you that a woman should never part from her husband whilst she can remain with him. This is generally the case; particularly so in such a case as yours, that is, in the case of a young handsome woman of lively imagination, . . . whose celebrity and superiority has necessarily created many enemies.[1]

And again on April 19, he advised her that she would certainly "act most wisely and prudently" by returning to Norton.[2]

Melbourne refused to see Caroline, however, and she found evidence in his letters that he was more interested in protecting himself than in assisting her. In the letters she wrote during the two months before the June trial, Caroline did not hestiate to remind Melbourne of his obligation to her or to set down her growing suspicion that he was not prepared to stand by her as she thought he should. She was undoubtedly mistaken in her repeated accusation that he no longer felt for her, but certainly the 1836 crisis signaled a marked cooling of the prime minister's ardor for Mrs. Norton.

1. Quoted by Perkins, *Mrs. Norton,* p. 86.
2. Ibid.

12

He has taken all my children from me! — You thought me causelessly irritated in the morning, when he said Miss Vaughan had advised me not to take Spencer out of town [in] such weather. *I knew my fool* better *than* you — *I* saw that some one had meddled in my home. In the evening he picked a quarrel with me about nothing, & then said the children shouldnt go, & forbid the servants to obey my orders. Next morning while I went to consult Seymour, he put them all into a hackney coach & sent them *to Miss Vaughan* who sent them to a house agent, and after 4 hours search & baffling, — when I *did* find them, this agent refused to let me even *see* them, & *called in the police!* I could hear their little feet running merrily over my head while I sat sobbing below — only the ceiling between us, and I not able to get at them! my little merry Briney! & poor Spencer who had been so ill and was to be so carefully muffled up to go down with me to the sea — all dragged about in damp hackney coaches to get someplace to hide them from their mother — as if while I & they are on the same earth they *can* be put where I shall not find them. I came away without being able even to kiss them & say good bye — if they keep my boys from me I shall go mad.

This is my Easter "that was to calm me & do me so much good." I have done nothing but cry since I saw you, but I have done weeping now, and we will see whose wit will cary [*sic*] them furthest, now that I know how to get at them.

I cannot write any more — write to *me* — there is more

comfort in a word of yours or in a look than in all that other people can do. I wish I had never had any children — pain & agony for the first moments of their life — dread & anxiety for their uncertain future — and now all to be a blank. He says I shall never have them again — he *wants* to drive me to do something which shall release him from the charge of "a wife & family" or he wishes to nail me to come back to him by keeping them as hostages.

I am very miserable. Send the enclosed to the physician[2] — he has been kind to me since I was a girl — he will write to me & see about them, & no one will prevent their seeing the doctor.

Yrs ever
Car

I have just got a letter *from my footman* to say that the children are taken to Grantley's at Wonersh, & to inform me that Norton has been enquiring whether he, the servant, ever remarked any familiarity on *Fitzroy Campbell's*[3] part, or any other gentleman who comes to the house. The man's letter is most respectful & well intentioned, but the disgrace of this will kill me — and my boys!

Thank God every one in the house hates him so they will all write & tell me what is done.

Brin & Seymour[4] will decide for me — The physician cannot see them there.

1. Frampton Court, the Dorchester home of Caroline's brother, Richard Brinsley Sheridan, and his wife, the former Marcia Grant. In March, 1836, Caroline planned an Easter visit with the Sheridans for herself and her sons. At the last moment, however, her husband used their eldest son's scarlatina as an

excuse to prevent his wife's proposed holiday excursion. When Norton had the boys incarcerated at the residence of Miss Vaughan's agent, Mr. Knapp, Caroline went to stay at Frampton Court, where she subsequently learned that her children had been taken to Wonersh Park. Caroline remained at Frampton Court until April 22.

2. Dr. Herbert. See above, Letter 9, n. 1.

3. Perhaps the editor of the popular anthologies, *The Beauties of the British Poets* (1824) and *Flowers of Literature* (1826).

4. Along with Sir James Graham, Caroline's uncle, her brother, Brinsley, and her brother-in-law, Lord Seymour, advised her and represented her in extensive negotiations with Norton's lawyers both before and after the trial.

Frampton. Monday. [*April 4(?), 1836*]

This is a *blank* day to me, for there is no post from town. I am worn out with pondering on my affairs, and with wondering why & how this sudden *crash* has come upon me. I have quite made up my mind what to do, and it is *this*. If tomorrow's post brings (as I suppose it *must*) the news that Sir W. Follett[2] thinks a divorce *impossible*, then I will write to Seymour & Graham & bid *them* pause: — and I will also write to Barlow,[3] the Clergyman whom we attend in town, to go and talk to Mr. Norton on this matter. N. is by way of being a *religious* man, & unless he is the greatest hypocrite in the world, this will have an effect on him. If Barlow's mediation succeeds, I will go back home *unconditionally*, for several reasons. 1st I perceive that N. is entirely guided by others, & those my foes, in this matter; consequently he certainly will never consent to *any terms* such as I originally proposed. 2ly I can always *leave* my home if I find it utterly unendurable and I shall have time so to pave & prepare the way for that step, (by acting for a year or so on *all the rules* on which so much value is set) — that when I do go, no one shall be able to say it is for this Man, or that Man, that we are parted. 3ly I shall be with my children without a struggle, & I shall baffle those who have planned all this against me.

If on the other hand N. acts as he has said; forces me to sue for alimony, & deprives me utterly of my poor boys — then I shall acquiesce *apparently* for a while; — write to Leopold to know if The Queen[4] would countenance me at Brussels, steal my children suddenly (every thing being well arranged before-hand) & go to Brussels — or, failing the advantage I have mentioned, to some other place, in Italy or Germany.

If he is induced to take a middle course & makes me an allowance, leaving me the care of my children, then it will depend materially on what *stand* is made for me, whether I shall remain in England, or go abroad. If you advise me in any way on these three points, pray do. No one knows what I have suffered, or the chilled, cold quietness, with which I am now writing. I regret in England only my family and yourself. *"My family"* will write to me & laugh among themselves as before — and *you* will find perhaps someone as willing to devote her time & thoughts to you, & more able to entertain you. This is a *triste* ending at seven & twenty!

I was looking thro some papers last night for N's own letters, shewing that we had *discussed* & settled *at the time* those causes of grievance which he starts [*sic*] now as new ones. I read some of his and also some of yours, and I could not help smiling (a bitter smile) at the reflection how very small a portion of our own very short lives a *single interest* is permitted to stand forward and obscure others, and above all how the one (as it is most falsely called) *master passion,* occupies a less time than any other interest; — here is a man, who was mad to marry me at eighteen, who turns me out of his house nine years afterwards & inflicts vengeance as bitterly as he can by taking away the children who were the offspring of that long desired union & cursing me *thro' them*. And here am I, appealing to you (with a mournful conviction of my own folly) to *try* & feel as much for me as you did when you *"could not think what had become of me because I had not written for three days."* Well, well — it is all a folly perhaps, only I cannot think what spell is on my life that it should *finish* so much sooner than others. Georgia is *beginning;* full of plans, full of far off hopes & views — Brinsley is *beginning*; looking joyfully forward to unaccomplished ends. *They* all talk & think of nothing but their future, and I alone

68

stand amongst them, looking back, far back, and thinking that if I could make my peace with God, it would be as well to die *now*, as to wait.

Yrs affect'ly
Cary

1. An excerpt from this letter initially appeared in my "Caroline Norton, Lord Melbourne, and the Custody of Infants: Fragments of a Correspondence," which the *Mary Wollstonecraft Newsletter* published in July, 1972 (1:1–8). Excerpts from Letters 15, 22, 23, and 29 were also printed in that article and are reprinted here by permission of the publisher.

2. Sir William Webb Follett (1798–1845) appeared as counsel for George Norton against Melbourne at the trial. Follett was solicitor-general under Peel, 1834–35, and again in 1841; he was appointed attorney-general in 1844.

3. The Reverend Mr. Barlow, rector of the Duke Street Chapel, subsequently consulted with George Norton, but his overture was unavailing.

4. Louise D'Orleans, first queen of the Belgians. See above, Letter 9, n. 8.

14

[*Frampton, April 1836*]

I have just got yr note. I had sealed & written the enclosed[1] before it came, but Barlow the Clergyman has been with me, and what with talking & weeping I forgot it had not been sent. You will see that some of it was *scratched over* — bear with me! forgive me if that part is cold & taunting — it is, believe me, my meaning what *I cd do for you* with what you shd do for me, that makes me perhaps exaggerate in expectation, when I appeal to you, what you should feel on that appeal.

Barlow has been very kind; he is going to try & see Norton tomorrow and I have written a few lines *to* Norton that Barlow may read to him. I have of course not mentioned *you*, I am *supposed*, & will to the last possible minute *appear*, ignorant of this new accusation.

I have offered a few short *reasonings,* & I have desired Barlow to let me if possible have an interview with him. I recoil from this burning disgrace, with an agony, which is perhaps a *triumph* to those who inflict it, but I will yet hope it may not be — I will hope to the last. N is unwilling, *most* unwilling *himself* to bring you forward. Grantley, & perhaps other Tories have urged him to do it.

I repent the imprudence in the enclosed of proposing *compounding* with N. I perceive *your* enemies join *mine. Do nothing* till you hear from me tomorrow, & for the present suppose us to be on *the point of reconciliation.* We have time before us. I think Barlow will do good. I dare say *even now*, all may end without scandal.

70

God bless you. I hope you will not be ill, now that I may not see you. Take care of yourself, & remember me *kindly*, are my two prayers.

Recollect the enclosed was written *before* this.

Car

1. This enclosure evidently was not preserved.

15

Grosvenor Square[1] *[late April 1836]*

I am anxious to know how you are, and I trust you will send word by the bearer of this. Mr. Barlow came and sate with me for nearly two hours this morning and told me all he had done, or rather attempted to do, in my favor. He described Norton's conduct as that of an ungovernable *child*; he would neither read my letter himself, nor hear it read; but foamed, and stamped, & rambled from one accusation to another so that it was impossible to make out what he wanted, or *who* he meant to attack. Barlow says it is his impression that Norton has come to no determination whatever & that he (Norton) evidently *disbelieves* my guilt himself, and talks of his being unable to back out because of his lawyers! He (Norton) told Uncle,[2] he would *marry again*, & have *other children*. Barlow told him I would resist a divorce by every means in my power, & that therefore he would only disgrace me & *himself* to no purpose; that I had said I would rather starve as N's wife all my life, than leave him free to give a step mother to my children.

Brinsley went to Dr Lushington,[3] who was ill, but will see him tomorrow. He and Sir J. Graham will see him *together*. Dr. L. is not to be *retained*, but *consulted*; & *then* (if he think it *impossible* to arrange matters in an amicable manner), he will be retained by Brin for me.

Dont on any account trust *Young*[4] about this affair. Norton has somehow drawn him into it, & he is a very mischievous man — more, I think, than you are aware. Till Lushington has been consulted, of course nothing can be known of their proceedings, but however it is to end I do hope & expect that I shall know certainly tomorrow whether N. *does* mean to try for a divorce & *who* against. Even *that* would be something, *now*, that I am so worn with suspense.

You talk of my bracing myself & resisting. Resistance is all in vain, for I am *in his power* — and as to nerving myself, *I cant do it* in a state of uncertainty!

I'm vexed & frightened about my children — the Grantleys are capable of any treatment towards them. I am exhausted *bodily*, by sleeplessness & crying, and my heart sinks & chills at seeing how little I am to *you*. I dont mean to vex you — I know you dont *want* to vex *me* — but every circumstance of this affair, (vexatious as it must be to any woman with an atom of feeling) seems *doubled* for me. There is not tenderness enough in the father of my children to make their presence anything but a *triumph* to him — to other men it would be a *memory*; — I am to be a childless mother & a disgraced wife for my *supposed power to charm* strangers, and yet the man whom I have been "charming" ever since I was two-and-twenty —

Well! I beg pardon. I dont want to torment you — all I say is, *worse* women have been better *stood by*.[5]

When Brin has seen Lushington — or whenever I have anything to tell — I will write — and do you just send me a line to say you are better — or *well* tomorrow.

God bless you.
Yrs Cary

I have just got your letter [endorsed]

1. Brinsley Sheridan kept a town residence at Grosvenor Square, where Caroline stayed during the final week of April, 1836, while she negotiated with her lawyers.

73

2. Sir James Graham. See above Letter 5, n. 1.

3. Stephen Lushington (1782–1873), the famed barrister. Caroline and her representatives sought Dr. Lushington's advice from time to time, both before the trial and during a period of several years thereafter. In 1816–17 Lushington had served as counsel for Lady Byron in her separation proceedings, and he was influential in persuading Byron to agree to a private settlement and a quiet separation. It was to Lushington that Lady Byron first revealed her suspicion of her husband's incestuous relationship with Mrs. Augusta Leigh. With Lords Brougham and Denman, Lushington was also retained as counsel for Queen Caroline in her 1820 divorce trial before the House of Lords. He was appointed judge of the Consistory Court of London in 1828, and he served as judge of the High Court of Admirality from 1838 until 1867.

4. Tom Young, Melbourne's private secretary, formerly purser on the duke of Devonshire's yacht. A man of coarse and familiar manners, Young was loyal and useful to his employer, but he was evidently not always honest or scrupulous (see Henry Dunckley, *Lord Melbourne*, p. 243).

5. In his letter of June 9, 1836, Melbourne responded to Caroline's recurrent charge that he regarded her plight with selfish indifference:

> I daresay you think me unfeeling; but I declare that since I first heard I
> was proceeded against I have suffered more intensely than I ever did in
> my life. I had neither sleep nor appetite, and I attributed the whole of my
> illness (at least the severity of it) to the uneasiness of my mind. Now
> what is this uneasiness for? Not for my own character, because, as you
> justly say, the imputation upon me is as nothing. It is not for the political
> consequences to myself, although I deeply feel the consequences that
> my indiscretion may bring upon those who are attached to me or my
> fortunes. The real and principal object of my anxiety and solicitude is
> you, and the situation in which you have been so unjustly placed by the
> circumstances which have taken place (quoted by Perkins, *Mrs. Norton*, p. 93).

During much of April, May, and June, 1836, Melbourne was indeed indisposed; as he suggests, his ill health apparently resulted from apprehension about the approaching trial.

16

I have your note. You need not fear my writing to you if you think it *commits you*. I *struggle* to think over all the fortuitous circumstances which make *your* position seem of more consequence than *mine*. I will not deny that among all the bitterness of this hour, what sinks me *most* is the thought of *you* — of the expression of your eye the day I told it you at D[ow]n[in]g St — the *shrinking* from me & my burdensome & embarassing [*sic*] distress.

God forgive you, for I do believe no one, young or old, ever loved another better than I have loved you. *I trust "to truth & you"* — that is I look forward with satisfaction & resolute content, to seeing you *defend* the action (*if* that cruel coward brings one) to the utmost of your power. I *trust* to your doing your best to clear yourself from the imputation of having loved me enough to be rash enough to commit yrself for me — I trust to your power, & *facts* to carry you thro'.

So far — so good! I will do nothing foolish or indiscreet — depend on it — either way it is all a blank to *me*. *I* dont much care *how* it ends. I have always the knowledge that you will be afraid to see as much of me — perhaps afraid to see me *at all*. I have always the memory of how you *received me that day*, and I have the conviction that I have no further power than he *allows* me, over my boys. *You* & *they* were my interests in life. No *future* can ever wipe out *the past* — nor *renew* it.

I will not write you again, because you seem to dread it. I'm sorry I have been a vexation to you — an embarassment [*sic*] to you. I would willingly have devoted my life to add to the comfort of yours & I earnestly hope there may never be hours which may *reverse* the importance of *real* & *false* gains & losses — & make you think of *me* with something of the gnawing pain I now think of you.

This is my last note till you desire an *answer* to any of yours. It is written in distress of mind which must excuse my fault or offence.

N. [orton] declines, (or rather his lawyer *for him*,) any discussion, so Lushington & Follett cant meet.

The Lansdownes[1] have been most kind.

God bless you.

Caroline Norton

---

1. Henry Petty-Fitzmaurice, third marquess of Lansdowne (1780–1863), and his wife, Lady Louisa Emma Fox-Strangways (d. 1851). Lansdowne was a Whig mainstay during the twenty years of Tory ascendency following the death of Charles James Fox. In the early nineteenth century his was the strongest voice in English government for state assistance for the purposes of education, and he was a lifelong supporter of Jewish and Catholic claims for equality in the political sphere. Lansdowne held Caroline Norton in high regard, and his friendship was invaluable to her in the years after the Norton-Melbourne trial.

17

[Grosvenor Square, late April 1836]

Mr. Norton is returned, but from the advice of my family, & the utter exhaustion I feel — and above all having secured the more calm & efficient intervention of Barlow the clergyman — I shall make no attempt at present to see him. Barlow was with him *alone*, an hour, and tho I cannot hope he had good news to tell me, since he has not *sent*, but allowed me to hear thro' a *third party* of his visit, still I think it *must* have had some effect.

When I think of all the harshness & cruelty — the coarseness & indelicacy — the spite & meanness, with which this affair has been conducted, by the *man who swore at the altar to love & protect me* — I *sicken* at the thought of returning even *for a time* to his house, but I shall see my poor boys — & then the *worst* will be over!

When I hear the results of Barlow's interview, I will let you know — & if *you*, or yr side, can make any discovery of what is going on, let *me* know; and at all events, let me hear *you are better*,[1] for every additional cause of anxiety adds to the weary sadness of my day, & the feverish restlessness of my sleepless nights.

I send Mrs. Shelley's letter to you wishing her success in her petition.[2]

My eldest boy came up with his father — how strange it feels that I should know he is in my — in *our* home — & yet feel *I* cannot see him! Pray write a kind line, if you are not ill! — I am, God knows.

Yrs, Car

1. See above, Letter 15, n. 5.

2. Following the death of her father, William Godwin, on April 7, 1836, Mary Shelley wrote to Caroline Norton, asking her to use her influence with the prime minister to have Godwin's pension continued to her stepmother. Melbourne subsequently informed Caroline that legally he could not award Mrs. Godwin any part of her late husband's income, but that he would find some other assistance for her. On April 21 Caroline replied to Mrs. Shelley's letter:

> I suppose Lord Melbourne proposed to make the Royal Bounty Fund available in the case of poor Mrs. Godwin, as in others where it has been difficult to arrange what should be done where a pension is impossible. Do not suppose that any worries of my own would ever prevent my doing what I could for any one, far less for you, of whom, though I know comparatively little, I have heard and thought a great deal (quoted by Perkins, *Mrs. Norton*, p. 90).

Melbourne did in fact make the Royal Bounty available to Mrs. Godwin for some years.

Caroline and Mary Shelley first met some time in the mid-1830s, evidently at one of Samuel Rogers's famous dinner parties. From the time of that initial introduction, Mrs. Shelley held Caroline in high esteem; and, in the months that followed Caroline's intervention in Mrs. Godwin's behalf, the two women grew to be intimate friends and confidantes. In the autumn of 1835, when Edward John Trelawny wrote to Mary Shelley of his fascination with Mrs. Norton, she responded: "I do not wonder at your not being able to deny yourself the pleasure of Mrs. Norton's society. I never saw a woman I thought so fascinating. Had I been a man I should certainly have fallen in love with her . . . . " (Edward John Trelawny, *Letters of Edward John Trelawny*, ed. H. Buxton Forman, p. 192).

78

NORTON IGNORED ALL PLEAS for a retraction of his charges and persisted in a plan which, if successful, would ruin Melbourne politically and blacken Caroline's name before the whole world. The Norton children remained confined at Wonersh, and Grantley refused to let their mother see them or communicate with them in any way. Once, at least, evidently during May or early June, Caroline actually went to Wonersh and endeavored to steal her sons away. She managed to get inside the house and actually carried Brinsley to the estate gates before Grantley caught them and prevented her desperate attempt.

By the middle of June, London seethed with excitement over Norton's suit. Nothing had so aroused the city since the divorce trial of Queen Caroline sixteen years before. The fate of the government, and indeed of the Whig Party, was considered to depend on the verdict, and Melbourne informed the king that he was ready to resign. William IV hated the Whigs and would have welcomed a change of government, but he detected a Tory plot and refused to discuss a resignation. "I will never countenance an attempt of any party to turn to its advantage an error of conduct of this description," he informed his advisors. "We have all had our faults in this way."[1] And the duke of Wellington, from the side of the opposition, encouraged Melbourne to hold his office.

Finally the fateful day arrived, and while Caroline waited at her mother's apartments at Hampton Court, Sir William Follett presented the case for the prosecution. Melbourne's counsel, Sir John Campbell, quickly discredited the testimony of several of Norton's household servants, who obviously had been bribed and coached by Lord Grantley. London gossip had raised the highest expectations of some correspondence found in Caroline Norton's desk; but Follett produced only a handful of prosaic letters, including three trivial notes to Melbourne, which proved absolutely nothing. The jury was unimpressed, and, without requiring to hear a single witness for Melbourne, they returned a verdict in his favor.

1. Newman, *Lord Melbourne,* p. 216.

18 Spring Gardens[1] *[June 1836]*

I have got your note — they kept me to dine here, seeing that being *alone* only increases the disposition to fret and fidget. I am sure when you reflect on all my conduct to you, you *cannot* think me selfish towards you — you *cannot* think otherwise than that I have been most willing to consider *myself last*, & you *first* — you *cannot* look back upon our intimacy and say that you have any reproach to make me —

For *this* reason you should be willing to bear with me now — you should *try* and repress any impatience you feel at being mixed up in my affairs — you should recollect (what you more than any one know,) that my chief thought has been you all thro' — that I especially told my Uncle & friends who were settling this matter for me, that the moment *your* name was brought forward (*if* it should so happen) they should give up *everything*, & take what terms N. [orton] pleased rather than vex *you*. And you *might* also consider that the *only reason* why your name *has* at length been resorted to, is because, (tho' lawyers & enemies have worked incessantly for three weeks), they find it *impossible* to prove familiarity of manner with *any other man*. Surely these considerations might suffice to make you *choke back* the anxiety to see me *"safely out of the house,"*[2] which wounds and pains me — which I feel I do not deserve — and which, worn as I am with suffering, only bewilders me more — if you knew all the struggle it was to go to you at all — all the pain it was to say it to you — all the hopelessness with which I set out — your manner would have been kinder than it was.

But I will not vex you further. I will *wait*, (with what *calmness* I can, after *three* weeks daily suspence & discomfort) and hope that what *was not*, cannot be proved — I have been to my own house — I find the witness[3] who will *swear to it*, a man who can be *proved* utterly unworthy of credit — but *habitual intimacy* is easily proved & supported. — I beseech you not to do anything without letting me know *what is to be* done — I shall write to you if you do not like to see me — I hope you will also write to *me*.

Pray think what it is to *finish all* at seven & twenty, and that on a false & cruel lie — let the thought give you that patience with me which fancy or passion cannot — and be kind, since your not *intending* that I should be a sufferer does not prevent my suffering.

Yrs, Car

---

1. For a short time during mid-June, 1836, Caroline took a room at Hill's Hotel in Spring Gardens, southwest of Trafalgar Square.

2. In defiance of Melbourne's mandate that she make no attempt to see him, Caroline went to his lodgings (probably at his private residence in South Street), shortly before the trial.

3. Fluke, the drunken coachman, who spent several weeks before the trial as Lord Grantley's guest at an inn near Wonersh Park (Acland, *Caroline Norton*, p. 89).

19

Monday 20 June [1836] Spring Gardens

In a couple of days, all cause for complaint, insult, or reproach, will be at an end, therefore I will not ask from what feature of the *past* you draw your expectation that I am likely to *disobey* a request of yours.

If all the world advised me not, & every friend I have, knelt to me to persuade me to a different line, I would do whatever you asked – or bid me do. I merely repeat my strong impression that you have ceased to feel the affection for me which you did. I will do anything on earth that *voluntary exertion* or sacrifice can enable me to do, & that *instantly* & *without demur.* It does not depend on voluntary exertion how one *feels* — I wish it did, — for my sake, not for yours!

It is the vanity of women (which always leads them to think their own an *individual & peculiar case*, & that they are to be treated better than their neighbours) which has misled me into a painful struggle of hope & fear, instead of quietly taking my place in *the past*, with your wife Mrs Lamb — & Lady Brandon [*sic*] —

I enclose Georgiana's copy of the agreement made, after some struggles, by Col: Stanhope[1] with N[orton]. You shall have the original letter *from Stanhope to me* early tomorrow — my solicitor has them all. The agreement, or rather proposal, was *not in N's handwriting* it was taken down by Stanhope in writing, sore against N's will, as you will see in the letter I mention. Norton objected to the clause which enabled me to see my children — & Stanhope *wrote* it, to prevent his backing out. He would have seen us all dead before he would have written it himself.

Observe — it was *after* all this, that the witness Fluke was brought forward, & just as arrangements (different from the proposed agreement) were about to be made by mutual consent between us. On that witness coming forward, N. told Sir J. Graham that he had altered his mind about *my guilt* & therefore declined further communication on the subject of a quiet separation. Aubrey Beauclerk[2] will have furnished Vizard[3] with the means of further proving how unworthy Fluke is of credit. He has been very good natured about it.

The robbery took place in August 1831.[4] You, yourself, sent me the police report —. Cummins had not then come to me. She came afterwards, on the birth of my beloved Brin, in November. The servants *in the house* were the witness, *John Fluke*, the witness *Elizth Brady*, the witness *Thomas Poulten* (in Captain Norton's[5] service), and a girl named Ellen Meek. *Mrs Moore* was the nurse, but she was with me.

A woman who has been questioned, (but I do not know if she is subpoena'd) married to a policeman, & called *Sarah Stirrup*, had *left* immediately before, & was *suspected*, & most harshly questioned in her own house by Mr. Norton. I enclose a letter written at the time to Charles Norton. It does not appear to me to be of much use, but it is the only one I can find. You will see how bad they *all* were. I also enclose your own letter at the time.

If you like to believe Wynford you can, & Cumberland[6] too. *I* dont, because I *know* that N *was* at Wynford's, & I know what Cumberland said at Londonderry's[7] — but I am glad they swear their lies to you because it shews they are convinced you will win the day. So far from losing sight of his dear ward for years, both N & I were invited to [illegible] *last February*, and only omitted the visit because I, being unwell & unhappy, disliked the thought of Lady Best's[8] vulgarity & stingy wretched house-keeping. N. has *always* been in the habit of going *there*, as I know to my cost, for they always contrive to sour his temper against me.

Lord Grantley never speaks of you but with affected contempt & gross abuse, & never *did* — nor have James & the rest of the family ever since *you refused that living.*[9] I wrote the circumstances yesterday to Vizard in the hope that *perhaps* it might be of service.

If there is anything else I can tell you, you will let me know, *without* accusing me of doing anything *"under a pretext"*. I do not wish to "abuse you" (it is a hard word). I may express myself strongly, because I do feel *most bitterly*, but that will not prevent my following to the letter any directions you may give, as you will find. It would indeed be a melancholy folly on my part to thwart or force you into measures from which yr whole soul revolts.

Yrs Caroline

Mr N & I have agreed to separate two or three times. Mrs C.[harles] Norton holds one agreement which her husband drew up with Seymour.

,1. Leicester Fitzgerald Charles Stanhope, later fifth earl of Harrington (1784–1862). Colonel Stanhope served with distinction in India, and in 1823 he went to Greece as agent of the English committee in aid of the Greek cause against the Turks. Stanhope worked for a time with Lord Byron, whom he met in Cephalonia. Unlike Byron, however, Stanhope favored the establishment of a Greek republic, and he was more sympathetic with the western Greeks than with Bryon's friend Mavrocordatos and the eastern Greeks. After Byron's death in April, 1824, Stanhope brought his body back to England. The Stanhopes were close friends of the Nortons, and during the spring of 1836 Colonel Stanhope attempted to serve as intermediary between Caroline and her husband.

2. Aubrey William Beauclerk (1801–54), M.P. for East Surrey from 1832 till 1837.

3. A junior counsel for the defense at Melbourne's trial.

4. See above, Letter 11. Evidently Melbourne suspected that the supposedly incriminating letters, then in the hands of Norton's counsel, had been taken during the 1831 robbery at Maiden Bradley.

5. Charles Norton (see above, Letter 7, n. 5).

6. Ernest Augustus, duke of Cumberland (1771–1851), a long-time nemesis to all Whig statesmen, was believed to be involved in the "plot," along with Lord Wynford.

7. Charles William Stewart, third marquess of Londonderry (1778–1854), ambassador to Berlin, Vienna, and St. Petersburg; he received the Garter made vacant by Wellington's death in 1852.

8. Lord Wynford's wife, the former Mary Anne Knapp (d. 1840).

9. The Reverend James Norton (1809–53) was another of George Norton's brothers. One of Melbourne's prerogatives as prime minister was the awarding of church benefices or livings. Apparently he had failed to grant a living to someone the Nortons favored, perhaps James Norton or some other member of the family.

20

Hill's Hotel. Spring Gardens. [*June 21, 1836*]

In obedience to your expressed wish, I send you Col: Stanhope's letter of the 8th of April, and my reply. I sent you Col: St's letter at the time, you will probably recollect it.

I saw Uncle Graham on my arrival here, (where by my lawyer's advice I shall remain till after the trial.) He said he had expected daily to hear from you, in compliance with your promise that *"you would consider, & consult, & communicate ultimately on the subject with him, which you thought was the object of your interview with him —"* that he had not heard a syllable and therefore could tell me nothing, and that he was unwilling to force himself *uninvited* upon you, altho' it was now the day before the trial & consequently your decision whatever it may be must be made, and he was very anxious to know what I wished him to do." I agreed that it was better not to force a visit, & said I would write to you. You do not like to be advised, or I would say "see him;" — not for *me*, for I perceive clearly how things will turn out, but that no one may think you *put them off* at the time of an earnest request, with a promise you did not intend to fulfill, of future decision & reply. Tomorrow is the day of trial.

It is the universal opinion that you will succeed — even one of their own attornies let out as much, to a clerk who repeated it to my lawyer.

You once said *to me* that in the event of N[orton]'s failing in obtaining a verdict you could "arrange with him" & "come to terms" — in short I forget the exact expression — except that he should "take me back". I therefore tell you that it is my intention, (on *the best legal authority Edinburgh contains*) to proceed for divorce against him in the Scotch Court, & that I have all the papers [now?] ready for that purpose as soon as he shall have failed here. So if it ever was your intention to communicate by attorney with him afterwards, it will not bind *me* in any way to come to terms with him. I thought I had better tell you this as you generally *act first*, and *then* let me know what has been done.

The bearer will bring any reply, either respecting Graham, or the enclosed papers, or any further request you may have to make to me — or if you do not choose to send by her, you can direct to me at *18 Spring Gardens* where I dine at *three o'clock*, or under cover to Bentick[1] if you prefer it.

I hope you are quite well now.

Yr Caroline

1. Mrs. Norton's friend, whose name and address Melbourne sometimes used, in the spring and early summer of 1836, to camouflage his letters to Caroline.

21

[18 Spring Gardens, June 21, 1836]

I am going to Hampton Ct with my Mother at 3 o'clk & shall stay there till something is settled. I will not say anything more to reproach or give you pain. I will not worry you. Only be well assured that you need not have shrunk. I would not have been any burden or trouble to you or to any other person, under *any* circumstances.

The fault is in *me* — I do not *attach* people. I have always thought so & said so. I did what I could for my husband. I was of great service, of great comfort to him. I nursed him devotedly at a time when many young married women would have shewn great displeasure & resentment. I thought I *owed* him to *replace* that love which is *in*voluntary, by all the cheerful effort which can so easily be made voluntarily. No man ever admired me *more*, or loved me *less*. I have been eight years his legal mistress & nothing more — no kindness — no tenderness, no *clinging* to the companion of younger days no sentiment for the Mother of his children. He thought me beautiful & full of talent but I did not *attach* him.

Well! I might say of *him* that he is incapable of such love, as I might have *earned* from another an. But *you!* I was of no service or comfort to you because I have never been in a position to render either — but my life has been divided (in *my* eyes) into the *days I saw* you & the *days I did not* — nothing else seemed of importance but you; your opinions, — even your *fancies* (for you *have* had them) have been laws to me. Yet you are not

89

attached to me — that is not a reproach — at least it is not meant as such.

As time wears on, & sobers *me*, I shall perhaps do you more justice and condemn my own wild expectations, rather than any part of your conduct towards me.

I was not two & twenty when you first visited me & I thought merrily & carelessly about you. I am six years older & I think sadly — perhaps something more! The time will doubtless arrive when I shall think *calmly & contentedly* — would it were come.

I trust & believe that as far as *you* are concerned, this *inquisitorial* proceeding will produce nothing. It will be a great relief to me to hear that they give up your name — *so* great, that I shd. feel *comparatively happy!* Farewell — in leaving town, I destroy at least *one* restless feeling — the knowing I am so *near* you & may not see you.

Caroline

THE TRIAL ITSELF was a deeply traumatic experience for Caroline. Naturally the public display of the details of her intimacy with Melbourne and the vulgarity of the charges, true or false, wounded her pride and self-respect. She was particularly pained by the testimony of Eliza Gibson, one of her former servants, who alleged that during the period of her employment Mrs. Norton was given to "painting" her face and to "sinning" with various gentlemen. Caroline was tormented by continued grief and frustration over the separation from her children and by the conviction that Norton intended to provide no support for her at all. Eventually he was constrained to offer his wife an allowance of £300 a year, but he still kept full possession of the children and denied Caroline access to them until late summer. Once by stealth she met her sons as they were taking a morning walk in St. James's Park. The malevolent Miss Vaughan found out about the meeting, however, and informed the boys' father, who dispatched them forthwith to Scotland and Lady Menzies.

Caroline's miseries were aggravated, moreover, by the belief that her lover — if indeed he had been that — had played her false. From the time of the first hint of Norton's action against him, Melbourne had refused to see her, and after the trial he sent her a stern note warning against any attempt to justify herself further by publishing their correspondence. He did write again on July 19, and on July 24 he addressed Caroline a guardedly apologetic letter, which professed his loyalty and his loneliness in the absence of her society and attributed her pique with him to "a little vanity and self-conceit."[1]

Caroline's biographers imply that Melbourne wrote frequently to her after the trial, expressing his regret and his sense of personal responsibility for her troubles; but her own incensed letters plainly accuse him of betrayal. Coupled with this sense of abuse and deception, her letters exhibit a feeling of pity and contempt for herself as a woman who must now take her place with those others — Caroline Lamb and Lady Branden — whom Melbourne had loved but in the end dismissed from his life as more bother than they were worth.

1. Perkins, *Mrs. Norton*, p. 107.

22

[*Hampton Court*] *July 1, 1836*

I did not write, because I was ill & weary — and it brings a choking in my throat and a pain in my heart every time I sit down to address you. If I had meant to cease writing I should at all events have replied to your note — but it is by no means *my* wish, Heaven knows, to widen the breach between us, by any *voluntary* act on my part. I am quite unhappy enough already, without that. I enclose you a note of Georgia's. I thought you might like to see what she says. It is unnecessary to say to *her* what I cannot help saying to *you* that the *distrust* (whatever the degree of it may have been), was caused, not *only* by the opinions & arguments of others, but by a very forcible remembrance of all you said & apparently *thought* about *Lady Brandon* [*sic*] — and which remained from that day to this, so heavily on my mind that it was in vain to bid me hope, or to say as they did "He has known *you* five or six years, it is not *the same thing*." I felt that it *was* the same thing — the wind-up & breaking off of an acquaintance which might have once seemed worth a sacrifice but which time had made you less anxious about. Well "it can never happen again" as the old Irishman said — when the last of his six sons died! — it can never happen again, for I shall never feel the same thing for any one else; and I suppose I shall learn to think of it all less bitterly — since no suffering lasts beyond a certain time. I "know the end" of all women's stories to be pretty much alike now; and shall not be a sufferer again for any love or trust I am likely to bestow on any human being.

I understand the objections to the prosecution for perjury. I believe it will not take place because they consider it necessary I should personally bear witness — a thing I will never do: but it certainly is a clear case, & it is hard to be made to appear like an Astley's[1] actress to gratify the spite of Ld Grantley. You know whether I left you to paint, but no one else can know it — except indeed one of the jurymen who had the advantage of knowing how much colour & [*sic*] I had, & how easily the complexion could redden or turn pale which was supposed to be so carefully prepared and if they had sate for a year instead of a day, & all the witnesses had been as respectable as they were infamous, *he*[2] would have stood to the verdict for you. I dare say it is partly vanity which made me feel so angry at what was alleged — it was *done* to mortify me & it *did* mortify me — but there was another reason. I was *prepared* to resist the accusation, or endure the false decision, of having *sinned* — & I believe many a better woman than I am, has committed such sin. I was prepared to have my feelings & conduct made the subject of public discussion — but I was *not* prepared for more than the *perversion of facts*. The loathesome coarseness & *invention* of circumstances — which instead of supporting an accusation of crime made me a shameless wretch — I was not prepared for. It was the difference between having an attachment out of one's own home, and being like a woman of the town.

Even my letters were garbled, *misdated*, & *chosen* to torment me. One sneering at Frank[3] — & one at Heath[4] the publisher (which is "taking the bread out of my mouth" as the servants say) and the last letter, which crowns all & which I suppose no other husband in Europe would have printed — since it is a reply to a bitter reproach & accusation of making him ill, by what he termed my "capricious refusal to live with him as a wife." Sir W. Follett said "a little domestic quarrel, in which she *owns herself in the wrong*" — Good Lord if people did but know the circumstances they were attempting to decide upon — it would make people very humble in giving an opinion! Miss

Vaughan we give up. Any counsel you give will be received as all you say has always been — as if there was no other person who had *a right* to contradict it — but how far *I* am to shape my own fate I scarcely know. Brinsley is very anxious to act — and by throwing the burden of my distress on him & Uncle, I have lost my free agency in some measure. If you had not kept me so *at arm's length* & written coldly & scoldingly when I was suffering, I never should have been either so miserable, or *required* to listen to all the opinions that only racked [and] tormented me. But that is all gone by now. I will send the memoranda on Scotch divorce when Brinsley sends it back. Nothing could be *begun* till September: if infidelity on Mr. Norton's part was proved, it would be decided in *twelve months* — if only desertion if would take four years from November.

Pray write to me when you can. I am ill one day & pretty well the next — only very low & unhappy. I never hear of the boys now Fitness[5] is gone. I applied to N. but he has not answered me.

Ever yrs Caroline

1. Astley's Amphitheatre, opened in 1798 by Philip Astley (1742–1814). the equestrian performer and producer of popular London entertainments.

2. This juryman eludes my identification.

3. Caroline's brother, Frank Sheridan.

4. Charles Heath (1785–1848), the engraver and publisher; best known for his engravings after Benjamin West.

5. A servant of Norton's who smuggled information to Caroline about her boys.

23

Friday [*Hampton Court, July 8, 1836*]

You need not have taken so very majestic a tone with me because you are now safe from all risk, & sitting in triumph at South St.

I never *threatened* to publish your letters — I said I *could* — and that therefore it was curious to see how you must have relied on my *bearing* the harshness you shewed me when you were uneasy, & which perhaps you might have spared me *today, that I am crushed.*

Considering that at least *you* know that instead of running up to *paint myself* in August September as deposed — I was *confined of my youngest child* — & was consequently *in my bed & on the sofa all* that time[1] — Considering that you only of all the world know how false the accusations are, of the cold & revolting indecencies I am accused of — & above all, considering that however *unwillingly* (both for *your own* sake & mine) yet still you *are* the cause of this blight upon my life — the cause of this public ribaldry & exposure in every way — the cause of all the filth & insult they could not draw down on me in *any other persons* name — tho they tried it; I say *considering all this*, there is hardly the man on earth who would not have written a kind word when the trial was over & asked how I was.

As to what I shall do after all these beastlinesses have been published — I dont know. I hope I may not live time enough to do anything. I have spit blood twice, for two or three days at a time, this last fortnight — & I am so weak I can scarcely stand.

My father was as strong a man as I *was* a woman, & yet he died after the same sort of accident[2] — I hope I shall go too — & so relieve you of your fears of committing yourself by too kind a correspondence with me—

In what capacity do you wish to be consulted — as a friend? Have you written as a friend? Have you shewn a friend's feeling? Have you shewn a friend's indulgence? Have you shewn a friend's sympathy? Have you not rather renewed the feelings of agony & shame with which I came down here & which was passing away a little, under the tenderness & coaxing & affected *joy* of my Mother & Sister. What have I ever done to you that *you* should grind me too? Have you *always* so preserved the inequality of age & understanding between us, that you should talk to me like God delivering the tablets of law to Moses? Can you give me back my children? Can you make all that burning shame pass away which has been the penalty for the amusement of *your* idle hours? Can you *un*do all the curse that is on me? Do not talk so proudly to *me*, who *thro' you* am destroyed who *by you* should have been comforted, & was not — who *to you* appealed in the bitterness of sorrow & received nothing but reproof. *God* knows it would be a lesson to many a woman if any one *could* read your letters from the first to the last — from the days you flattered me till the days you rose to fling stones at your own clay idol & break it; to prove to it that it was unworthy your worship —

I *was* satisfied with the result — my great fear was the cutting the damages to a farthing — an *acquittal* it is not in human nature not to rejoice at. There were but two things (beyond the grossness) which I was not satisfied at; one, that the Attorney Genl.[3] added to your solemn & *sufficient* assurance *"that you had not sinned with me"*, "nor in any way abused her husband's confidences" & the other, that he said it was *fact* that there were many other gentlemen equally long & equally often "cloistered" with me "as his Client" — However Thesiger[4] & he did their best for me.

May I ask what steps I have yet taken either on my own or others' suggestion? On the contrary I have been waiting till this was over to take any steps at all. All that *you* asked of me I did & nothing more—

In conclusion, I beg to say (if indeed it is not an *excuse* for breaking with me) that I can bear what I conceive to be a want of generosity in others, without *revenging myself* and that tho' when I look back on the days when your letters were written it seems almost *miraculous* that they came from the same man who writes today — when I look at their length, — the playful eloquencies — the interest in little things that interested me — the feeling & the beauty that runs thro all — you need not fear that the eyes of strangers shall ever profane lines I was so glad to get — or that others shall sit judgement on them, and decide *for how much or how little* of your *temporary regard* I cast my youth's hopes away. Others (perhaps as unhappy) have preceded me — others as unhappy may succeed me — but no one either in the past or the future will have loved you more earnestly, more completely — & I may say more *steadily* than the woman whose threat of passion you pretend to fear — & who has been made to appear a painted prostitute in a Public Court before a jury of Englishmen — for the sake of an acquaintance with one who did not think it worth while to ask after her the next morning!

Caroline

I believe I shall do nothing — I will let you know if anything is proposed. *Pray* do not write harshly — *pray* do not! I had rather be forgotten. I have not deserved it — & it kills me.

1. During the trial Eliza Gibson specifically referred to Caroline's flirtations during August, 1833, the month she gave birth to her youngest son, William.

2. Tom Sheridan died in September, 1817, evidently of "consumption," at the Cape of Good Hope where he was serving as colonial paymaster.

3. Melbourne's chief counsel, Sir John Campbell, later first baron Campbell (1779–1861); attorney general from 1834 until 1841. A liberal M.P. for Edinburgh for many years, Campbell became lord chancellor in 1859 and held that office until his death.

4. Sir Frederick Thesiger, later first baron Chelmsford (1794–1878). Thesiger appeared for the defense, with Serjeant Talfourd and Sir John Campbell, at the Melbourne trial. He was attorney general under Peel, 1845–46, and again in Derby's administration in 1852. Later Thesiger twice served as lord chancellor, in 1858–59, and from 1866 until 1868.

24

Wednesday [*Hampton Court, July 13, 1836*]

"Between us two let there be peace!" is all I can say — it is vain to dispute whose sentences were *hardest* — the difference between us is that *you never wrote a kind one* — & *I too many needlessly unkind* — (and often the reflection rather of the thoughts of others than of my own). Years will go by in vain for me & *my* disappointment. *You* will forget your annoyances: — *you* have been *angry* — I have been, & *am miserable:* — which of us has the advantage?

You wish to be told what is intended. It is proposed to prosecute the witness Gibson for perjury[1] — as I was confined to my room those months she mentioned as being occupied *painting* & *sinning*.

It is proposed to prosecute Miss Vaughan for defamation. I do not know if any thing is thought of against Grantley &c.

The attempt to obtain a Scotch divorce stands over. I will send you all the memoranda. I have no heart, or energy to *copy out* or make extracts; if it bores you you need not read it — it is only sent in compliance with yr wish.

Mr. Bentick[2] is going to Spain. I do not see why your letters need go under cover but if it must be so send them to Col. Stanhope 6 Hanover Square. I too, would have preferred *any* conversation to some of the letters — & I should think *if* you consider it so impossible to see me again that you might write more at length — but I dont press it — it is all hopeless together & from my soul & most earnestly I wish I were in my grave—

Mr. Cowper[3] came down here. I had rather he had not because I have heard all he said against me at the time — but I did not shew it in my manner — & I suppose I am to be thankful for people's civility, *now* —

God bless you. I would write more if I could write any thing to please you, but the purpose & spirit of my life is gone & I can do nothing.

Bentick will take this to town — & will be there till Saturday.

Yrs Caroline

1. See above, Letter 23, n. 1.

2. See above, Letter 20, n. 1.

3. Perhaps George Augustus Frederick Cowper, later sixth earl (1806–56), eldest son of the fifth earl Cowper and Melbourne's sister Emily. Cowper was M.P. for Canterbury, 1830–34, and lord lieutenant for Kent from 1846 until his death. Or, possibly, his brother, William Francis Cowper, afterward Cowper-Temple (1811–88), lord of the admiralty from 1846 until 1855, when he was appointed under-secretary for home affairs.

25

Hampton Ct. Tuesday [late July 1836]

Do not be impatient at my writing; Georgia will send the note under her seal, from her house; therefore the knowledge that I have written is confined to yourself. I think I have a right to ask you, if you, on your side, have heard any thing or done anything more in this affair. The Salisburys[1] said a note of yours was in the hands of lawyers, but they did not say who it was written *to*. Uncle Graham heard Ld Salisbury say so. . . . *pray* tell me if anything has been done. Do not let a selfish fear so get the better of your noble and generous nature.

The day will *come*, without your anticipating it, when one of us may no longer communicate with the other. Forbidding me to write after being in the habit of hearing from or seeing you so constantly, gives me a feeling as if you were *dead*, & adds one *needless* misery to what I am enduring. You risk nothing *writing to me*, and if you *think you do*, send yr note to Georgia as if you were not sure of my direction, & she will forward it to me.

You owe me this much kindness. I was fairly out of my scrape, one quarter of an hour before they brought a witness against *you*. Men are not easily touched, or I wd send you my letters to Stanhope to prove how anxiously I dwelt on their avoiding *your* name as if that was all that seemed of consequence in my *wreck*. I have behaved with little selfishness *to you* dear Lord — I have not deserved it *from* you. I hope you are well in health.

Cary

102

1. James Brownlow William Cecil, second marquess of Salisbury (1791–1868), and his first wife, Frances Mary (d.1839), the daughter and heiress of Bamber Gascoyne of Childwall Hall.

26

Thursday night [*Hampton Court, late Summer 1836*]

I send you a letter from Castlereagh.[1] I have scratched thro' the *preface* of lamentation & consolation, as being out of your *line*. — "Old and young Stagers"[2] take different views!

Norton has the same feeling as *you* about my letters. When the clergyman[3] said he had one from me in his pocket, Mr. Norton was quite alarmed, stretched his hand for the bell-pull, & said "Then Sir I cannot see you without *witnesses*."

It is to be hoped as this note "goes off" before any one is stirring (probably) in *your* home, or the houses of your *neighbours*, that you will master courage to face it & read it thro — Seriously I am ashamed of the coldness & terror you always shew at those times when other friends rally round one. It was the same when Brinsley married, and I was abused for it;[4] it was a *vexation* to me *then* — but not so good a lesson.

It would be very inconvenient for you as a public man, if all your party were equally inclined to stand behind the hedge, instead of "leaping over it." I have one of your old notes, describing yr disinclination to speak on some debate, in which you say [scratched out]. I quote wrong, — and enclose your note (too often read to be unremembered by me, even if you are afraid to return it!). I send it you only to prove that you need not give your "fear" any other name, such as *caution*, *prudence*, &c &c not for the rest of its contents, tho in that one note lies the key to much of the inexplicable folly of feeling I have from time to time been guilty of — including the scene with E. Eden,[5] at

Lansdown [*sic*] House, which you thought so dull without me while I was a *novelty*!

Well! You cant fasten a plucked flower on its stalk again — & *that* is over.

The more I reflect, the more *unnecessary* & *unkind* it seems that you should not write at this moment — but I cannot alter by argument or complaint what is in *your nature*. Nor can you alter mine. Even if every one did not stand amazed at the idea of your declining to write or be written to — I could not resist sending C[astlereagh] 's letter. I cant rest or sleep — the moment I get drowsy a strange fancy that I hear the stirring of a tea-cup & that they are poisoning my boy, comes over me — I dread the night — & my room, in which I am to spend the long pause between two heavy days, seems strange & dreary. To this wakeful state you owe this note — if *you* have slept tolerably well you will order the cheerfulness of your morning to forgive the irritableness of my night. Adieu!

When it suits you, let me have my notes again.

1. Charles Stewart, third marquess of Londonderry (see above, Letter 19, n. 7). Like his half-brother, Robert, second marquess of Londonderry, Charles Stewart was also known as Viscount Castlereagh.

2. The allusion is probably to Samuel Butler's *Hudibras*, part ii, canto I, ll. 297–98: "I've heard old cunning stagers/Say, fools for arguments use wagers."

3. The Reverend Mr. Barlow. See above, Letter 13, n. 3.

4. In 1835 Caroline's brother Brinsley eloped with and married Marcia Grant, the only daughter and heiress of Sir Colquhoun Grant, a Waterloo veteran and owner of considerable estates. Her father, after fighting a duel with Lord Seymour over the affair in the summer of 1835, threatened a suit against the Sheridan family for conspiracy.

5. See above, Letter 6, n. 3. Caroline and Emily Eden had more than one "scene." The encounter at Bowood (Lansdowne House) apparently took place in December, 1833; but in a letter which Violet Dickinson dates " [July 1833]"

Mrs. Norton expressed regret to Lord Auckland for ungracious deportment toward his sister on another occasion:

> As you are the only person in your family who have not "cut" me, perhaps you will allow me to apologise *through* you, to your Sister, for my rudeness last night.
>
> Say that, as far as concerns her, I consider my conduct on that occasion vulgar and unjustifiable, and that I beg her pardon. Yesterday was a day of great vexation and fatigue — which of course is no excuse in the eyes of strangers (whatever it may be in my own), for rudeness and want of temper. I am very sorry. My apology may be of no value to her; but it is a satisfaction to *me* to make it (Dickinson, *Miss Eden's Letters,* p. 227).

27

[16 Green Street,[1] *late Summer 1836]*

I have been reading the debate of last night[2] — it is the first thing for *three weeks,* that has made me forget my own affairs for a while. I see you were beat — but it will only make the struggle more determined. Let me know that you were not the worse for the fatigue & late hour of breaking up.

Brinsley is gone to Lushington.[3] My Mother has written, earnestly to urge me, *"if* it be *true,* what is alledged [*sic*],— to inform "Brin & Seymour of the fact, — to be sincere with *my own friends* — , and to "consider that a false defence will only aggravate my case." Nothing can vex me, more than I *am* vexed, and I know she disbelieved me all along, so it makes little difference, and in the sight of Heaven my crime is the same as if I had been yr mistress these five years, so I dont wonder or complain. I remember you yourself rebuked once the stress we women lay, upon what we call our "actual innocence", and made several pertinent observations on the subject.

He has ordered the youngest child to go by the name of *Charles* — it was christened William-Charles-Chapple — the affectation & insincerity of the whole thing makes my heart *burn.*

The servants tell me he eats, drinks, & sleeps as usual — has little dinner parties *with his lawyers,* in *the drawingroom* and puts any letters of evidence & consequence into an American writing desk, which *Fitzroy Campbell* gave him when they were friends! My maid said, "oh Ma'am we *wondered* at him, *preferring* to live in the drawing room, where *you* was always sitting when you was at home, and keeping that desk that he ought to throw into the fire if he really thought those things of you."[4] Even the uneducated coarseness of *their* minds, revolts at the cold brutality of *his*.

All the *petty* things he could do to spite me, he has done. We used to dispute about a dentist being allowed to *gold wire* Spencer's jaw (he is underjawed). I had a *horror* of this and said it never should be done. He took him yesterday — had it done — & merely remarked "I can do what I please *now* with you, my boy."

I had a few little memorandums & fooleries of by gone days, in an M.S. book which Leveson Smith[5] *left* me. There was poetry in it — & laments — & follies. He knew I cared violently about it — he knew it belonged to the years when I did *not* belong to him — & he *wrenched off the locks* off that, & a little *diary* also given me by Leveson.

He asked all the servants whether they had not remarked my poor Brin's likeness to you — they said "yes; he is more handsome & cheerful than the other children, & he had [*sic*] got something of my Lord's manner; especially for a day or two after he happens to see my Lord, he's very like". "Well isnt that enough to convince you — didnt you think all along that he was *his* child?" Now mark the answer of a *servant* to a man who is called a *gentleman*. "No Sir, we none of us thought it, because *the Mother would never have let a joke be made about the likeness,* if there had been a *reason for it*."

If I had had to defend *myself* — I know no better answer!

I cannot tell you how this tortures me. A story of Mrs. Gores[6] haunts me in which the man *keeps* the child out of revenge but yet believes it another's — & ill-uses it till it dies.

He desired Brin to tell him the truth about *me* or he would lock him up in a dark room for a week — Poor Briny — poor Briny he looked round the room fearfully & reddened & then he said — "Mamma wont *let you* lock little Briney up" —

I've told them to tell me nothing more that I maynt go frantic before it is settled — and yet I cannot help asking questions every five minutes. Spencer was taken to Lincoln's Inn, to the lawyers, yesterday.

And all this time you wont see me — and God knows, with your ways of thinking when I shall see you again.

Send me a line!

Car

1. Approximately a month after the trial Caroline left Hampton Court to share a house in Green Street with her half-uncle, Charles Sheridan. Apart from brief visits with her mother and with other relatives, Caroline remained at 16 Green Street until the autumn of 1839.

2. Undoubtedly parliamentary debate over the Irish Municipal Corporations Bill, which was passed by the Commons in June, 1836, and was subsequently rejected and returned by the House of Lords. Proposed revisions and amendments to the bill, which provided for parliamentary regulation of Irish municipal corporations and borough towns, occupied Commons during much of the last two weeks of July. Melbourne backed the Whig proponents of the bill, and Wellington led the Lords in opposition.

3. Dr. Stephen Lushington. See above, Letter 15, n. 3.

4. During the spring of 1836 George Norton included Fitzroy Campbell in the list of men he suspected of illicit relations with his wife (see above, Letter 12).

5. Leveson Smith (d. 1827) was the younger son of Robert Percy (Bobus) Smith and Caroline Vernon and also the nephew of the Reverend Sydney Smith. As particular friends of Lord and Lady Holland, the Bobus Smith family was included in the most exclusive circle of the Moderate Whig camp, of which Holland House was the social and political center.

6. Catherine Grace Frances Gore (1799–1861), the novelist and dramatist. Mrs. Gore published about seventy works between 1824 and 1862, including the novels *Manners of the Day* (1830), *Mrs. Armytage* (1836), and *The Banker's Wife* (1843).

URING THE EARLY AUTUMN OF 1836 Caroline began to go out again, and she occasionally gave small dinner parties at Green Street for Samuel Rogers, Abraham Hayward, and other particular friends. Restless and preoccupied, however, she found little pleasure in society and directed much of her energy to the completion of *A Voice from the Factories*, which was accepted by John Murray before the end of the year. Also that winter, with the aid of Serjeant Talfourd, she began her long battle for legal reform of the rights of mothers with the publication of a pamphlet entitled "Separation of Mother and Child by the Custody of Infants Considered."

Caroline and Norton had several painful interviews during the first three months of 1837. Norton declared himself willing to recall the boys from Scotland provided his wife agree to a permanent allowance of £200 a year — half the sum Melbourne had earlier advised Caroline she ought to have. Against her lawyers' recommendation, Caroline decided to accept the proposal; but, nevertheless, negotiations again broke down. Meanwhile, Melbourne remained aloof and detached, refusing to write to Caroline and seeing her infrequently and with the greatest reluctance. Despite his attempts to discourage correspondence, however, she evidently wrote to him constantly, grumbling about what she saw as callous selfishness and careless insensitivity to her plight.

By his own frank admission, Melbourne habitually avoided anything and anybody that threatened him with unpleasantness, and he must have found Caroline's perpetual attempts to regain his attentions exasperating. Caroline was only too aware of how uncomfortably her querulous letters were received, and one suspects that her often theatrical complaints were encouraged by that knowledge. As time passed, she grew increasingly resentful of Melbourne's life apart from her, and she conceived his female friends, who had taken her place both in his company and in his affection, to be her overt enemies. This jealousy, coupled with her compulsive desire for acceptance in London's most proper drawing rooms, and indeed at court as well, soon occasioned more wounds to Caroline's pride and further proof to her of Melbourne's bad faith.

28

[16 Green Street] March 6th [1837]

Don't be provoked with me! I know I asked for it myself and made up my mind to do so before you came — but now, somehow, it weighs upon me. It has haunted me all night, & I have a *paid-off, cast-off* feeling.

It is quite possible that if I ever *do* get my boy, I may request the same thing again and you will bear patiently what may *look* very like caprice, but certainly is not. At present I feel as if I had voluntarily raised one more *distance-post* between us.

And now if I copy the words of one of your old notes it is not in the spirit in which I have done so before — not as an *off*ence but as a *def*ence. I have always had the greatest horror of your thinking I was more forward than I should be, and what between that fear & other feelings, I have I dare say, like most people, who struggle with contrary impressions, done exactly the things I should not — but when you say as you have done once or twice "I always thought it an imprudence coming to S[ou]th Street." You lay to my charge the seeking you whether you desired it or not. I copy your words *exactly*. "I have been in despair today at not seeing you but I know it is a long way and a difficult operation — if you *can* continue to call, the later the better, as a number of people come to me for one reason or other."—

I admit I may have come when you did not want me, but that was like all the rest, *after* you yourself had taught me to wish it. *Then* it irritated and made *you* anxious to miss me for a few days — and *then* I came more to please *you* than to please myself —

now it breaks my whole life *not* seeing you and you come,
unwillingly, to satisfy *me* — and yet I am the younger & should
have been the likelier to alter.

I wish you would call *once,* on your birthday, the 15th—

Yrs ever
Caroline

29

[16 Green Street] March 17 [1837]

The *immaculate* & *irresponsible* Magistrate of Whitechapel[1] still hangs fire. He is probably afraid, by the ease with which his allowance was accepted that he has offered *too much,* & is concocting a plan by which he may propose £100 a year. I am daily more & more of Georgia's opinion that *men* have no real feeling. While they are in love they are kind, & when that noble passion has burnt out, they are brutes — like iron, they are only malleable in a state of fusion; — you cant bend a *cooled* man.

Here are *you* now, — (for I am obliged to allow so much comparison between your nature & the Irresponsible, —) while you were in the *malleable* state, you write [*sic*] all sorts of laments "you are gone" — "alas! I am old, & at my advanced time of life one cannot replace an object of unceasing & anxious interest" — "I went to Lord Hill's[2] breakfast — they *told me* it was pleasant but I could not find it so" — "I looked for *Miss Armstrong* but could not see her" — "I hope you feel an interest in the small details but perhaps I am deceived by knowing how every trivial circumstance about *you* interests *me.*" "I was very melancholy all yesterday after yr departure. I knew I should feel it a great deal, but did not think I should feel it so much as I do." &c &c &c, &c & frequent repetitions of the *extreme old age* you had arrived at.

This was when you were *malleable*, & could be made into a horse-shoe & nailed to the threshhold to keep away ill luck — but lo! as time rolls on, the mournful laments over me & your own *septuagenaire* feelings, cease. You become a *young* man — a fine bright bar of iron — a poker, resolutely stirring up a fire in people's houses, and only warming the tip of its own cold nose in the blaze. No longer "unable to replace objects of perpetual & anxious interest," and more fortunate than Virgil who was chopped up & renovated in vain,[3] you run about to Stanhopes[4] Litchfield[5] Fox Lane's[6] (not to count sundry acknowledged Murrys, Keppels, Sinclairs, & Smiths,) with the buoyancy of a boy, and the carelessness of a greyhound: — (the only dog besides yourself who cannot attach himself to *any one person*, but to the cushion where he habitually rests & the house where he is accustomed to be fed.) Fie on such love say I!

> The Pilgrims to a *single* shrine
> Bear far the destined treasure—
> Coldly their stedfast ears decline
> The truant call of pleasure, —
> And faithfully they win their way,
> With steps that never falter—
> Their hearts are fixed the gift to lay
> Upon *one* sacred alter!—
> Far different they who wander by,
> Each chance-met shrine adoring,
> With frozen prayer, & careless sigh,
> A hundred saints imploring;
> The murmur of *their* mocking call
> Is faintly breathed to many,
> But ah! too poor to furnish *all*,
> *They leave no gift at any.*

———————

Considering you destroy my letters, it is a pity I waste even *this* poetry upon you. If I could find a man of the present day who could write & read, & who did not carry a comb & a box of pink lip-salve in his coat pocket, I would not trouble you — but there are none such.

I believe I shall be going out of town on Tuesday.

There is a friend of Charlie's,[7] a goodlooking, tall officer named *Cole*,[8] who was going to an auction in Dublin; he was stopped by the door-keeper. "How *dare* you stop me, Sirrah?" "Faith, and its me *orders*." "Your orders — to stop *me*!" "Yes plase [*sic*] your honor — for me orders was, to stop all *mane-looking* fellows from coming in, in case they'd only stop up the way & buy nothing." I tell you this, because it is St Patrick's day, & because Charles has just told it to me — the *joke* lies, in the exceeding satisfaction the insulted Cole is supposed to feel in his own appearance.

You have never been at Lady Minto's[9] since *I* went. I cannot admire your taste. You always went *till* I came out — if you mean to sit at home, or with one of these women, for fear of meeting me at a party, things are come to a pleasant pass. . . .

God I believe this is the last note I shall write you — it troubles me all this shuffling & outwitting me — all this carelessness & Frederickism[10] — it is better to be nothing at all.

1. George Norton held the magistracy in the police court of Whitechapel from 1831 until practically the end of his life.

2. Rowland Hill, first viscount Hill (1772-1842), general; second in command of the occupation army in France from 1815 till 1818 and commander-in-chief in England from 1825 till 1839.

3. The allusion is to one of the numerous sagas concerning Virgil the Necromancer, a composite figure derivative of the Latin poet and some five other *legendary* Virgils, and known to the Middle Ages and the Renaissance as a poet, seer, priest, and magician. In the Dutch translation of the sixteenth-century French romance *Les faictz merveilleux de Virgille* appears for the first time the story of Virgil's abortive attempt to prolong his life. According to the Dutch writer, Virgil ordered a servant to cut him up and place him in brine, promising that he would be rejuvenated in nine days. On the seventh day, however, the emperor forced Virgil's servant to reveal his master's whereabouts, thus interrupting the magic and preventing Virgil's resurrection.

The sorcerer who attempts resuscitation in such a fashion, either upon himself or others, is a familiar character in story subsequent to the Virgilian romances. The classical tale of Medea and the daughters of Pelias is likely the original for this motif.

4. Melbourne was a frequent guest at Chevening, the home of Philip Henry Stanhope (see above, Letter 3, n. 5). Stanhope's wife, Catherine Lucy (d. 1843), daughter of first baron Carrington, was an intimate friend of Melbourne's and a frequent target for Caroline Norton's jealous accusations during the late 1830s. Lady Stanhope, who at one time was almost certainly the mistress of Melbourne's brother Frederick, was a woman who might well have appealed to both men. Lady Holland in 1824 described her as "very amusing, gay and original, *not of the best polish*, but still very sprightly . . . and highly coloured in her stories" (Elizabeth Holland, *Elizabeth, Lady Holland to Her Son, 1821–1845*, ed. the Earl of Ilchester, p. 32).

5. Probably John Litchfield (d. 1858), of the privy council office, husband of Harriet Litchfield (1777–1854), the Shakespearean actress.

6. James Fox-Lane (d. 1821), of Bramham Park, the friend of George IV.

7. Caroline's brother (see above, Letter 8, n. 4). Evidently Charles Sheridan resided at Green Street with Caroline and their uncle during much of 1836 and 1837.

8. Probably Arthur Lowry Cole, later colonel, son of Sir Galbraith Lowry Cole (1772–1842), the governor of Mauritius and the Cape of Good Hope. Colonel Cole commanded the seventeenth regiment throughout the Crimean War.

9. The London residence of Lady Mary Minto (d. 1853) and her husband, Gilbert Elliot, second earl of Minto (1782–1859). Lord Minto succeeded to the post of first lord of the admiralty in 1835, and he continued to preside over naval affairs until the dissolution of Melbourne's second administration in 1841. Minto was lord privy seal from 1846 until 1852.

10. Melbourne's brother Frederick, later Lord Beauvale and third viscount Melbourne, was a notoriously cavalier ladies' man. As a youth he was involved with the infamous Harriet Wilson, and he occupies a prominent place in Miss Wilson's *Memoirs* (1825) as one of her early "protectors." In 1841, when he was sixty, he married the Prussian countess Alexandrina Julia, a woman thirty-six years his junior.

117

30

[*16 Green Street*] *March 19* [*1837*]

I must beg that you will send word by the bearer whether you received my note of Saturday, as in spite of the carelessness of other people's feelings it is your pleasure to shew, when they are apparently *nonentities*, I should wish to ascertain whether that note went to *you* or to some one else.

There is not a human being (of those who are intimate enough to express an opinion) who does not join in denouncing as heartless & cold blooded the manner in which you parade yourself among my acknowledged & open foes, & who do not wonder at it.

You are also much mistaken if you think the circle of flattery & intrigue in which you pass your time, adds to your political importance or stability. There is not a day that some incautious or uncertain speech of yours is not repeated — a fact which I dare say you utterly disbelieve, & will continue to disbelieve till the *necessity* which checks the wavering & discontented portion of your supporters passes away, & you perceive as an individual, what you refused to see as a minister.

There are two things you are impatient of, *besides* contradiction — *distrust* & *ridicule*. I think you are earning both, & so would you, if you heard as plain words as I do. You are in a set where, tho' *individuals* may like you, all you say is caught at & perverted—

You may believe this or not — it is no affair of mine — on the contrary it should be rather a triumph that those you *chose* to fling yrself upon, only *injured* you — since you are utterly indifferent as to their injuring me. I tell it you, & if you like rather to plume yrself & think it merely said out of jealousy — do. Some one may make a leap past *you*, as well as past Ld Grey.[1]

In what is private, & regards myself, I have no more *words*. The opinion of others justifies me in feeling a sorrowful resentment, & I am glad of it, *not* because I desire to hear others find fault with you, but because it convinces me that what you would fain persuade me & yourself is captiousness of temper, is no more than the natural provocation all must feel, whose hearts are not seared by custom or cold by nature.

Pray send me word merely whether you received that note.

Yrs C

1. Earl Grey's Whig reform ministry was compelled to resign in 1834, following the implication of his Irish secretary, Edward Littleton, in secret negotiations with Daniel O'Connell. Grey was succeeded by Melbourne.

31

I do not know what you mean by *my* making you ill. From first to last I have done what you wished done — as much since I felt that I was of little or no value in your eyes, as when I thought I came far before & beyond yr other women — when I thought I was the object of as *near* a real preference as you could feel.

From the last evening I ever saw you, (which wound up with a request of assistance *from* me instead of any promise *to* me) I have done my best to satisfy you. I might have done it with more temper — without reproach — without bitterness. I regret that the restlessness of my nature prevented this — but let it be done how it might, it *was* done, — nor, had I been left entirely to myself, & not advised, adjured, sneered at, & maddened, by the contrary opinions among those who cared for me — would you have found me unwilling to pass over what after all is yr nature & so cannot be helped.

Lately circumstances have been told me — pressed upon me, proved (as far as anything is proved in this world) which make our "friendship" a burning insult to me. There are insults women are very slow to forgive — and I think yr connection with Lady Stanhope[1] is one. I wrote to you about it & you say *you* will look over the expressions of *my* letter!!

You will never make me like those women. I have a full recollection of Lady Brandon [*sic*] & the small space her supposed discomforts occupied in yr mind. I wish I had never known that *experience by proxy*.

You sit among my foes & make them yr best friends. They know they may act as they please & *you* will not resent it, and Mrs Fox[2] gives "commission" dinners at yr house.

All this does very well if you could *stab* me instead of only making my heart-ache — but so, while I breathe, it shall *not* be well. I looked to you for protection — for kindness — for sympathy. I perceive nothing but shrinking & a vague desire to be rid of me all together.

You will never succeed. We may be foes — for if you sow the wind, you will reap the whirlwind — but you will never make me *quiet & indifferent*. It all hangs on a thread — it wants but a little to make me utterly careless of *what* may be the effect of my own destiny or that of others — it wants but a little to make me careless of disgrace, ruin or life itself. They bid me be quiet & thrust a card for some party into my hand. But it will not do. That was *a part* of my life — it will not make a life of itself. You will drive me mad and for my madness you may thank yourself.

Stay away or come — choose your own way — I have not the decision to make — nor the responsibility. I dont ask you to come *twice*. I too hoped there would be no more bitterness, but hope is a thing banished from my vocabulary. You have made two or three unhappy destinies — look to mine and let yr women look to it. There are plenty who have been willing to perish themselves in springing a mine. I did not wish to charge either tone or feeling to you, & if my life *is* to wind up in a quarrel with you, I do not care how soon it finishes.

1. See above, Letter 29, n. 4.
2. Mrs. James Fox-Lane; see above, Letter 29, n. 6.

32

I have just returned from Ly Mintos.

I am reminded, by seeing Ellice[1] there to tell you that I never asked you to call *alone*. You chose him — he is good natured — let the end & the beginning be of a piece, & bring him with you.

You will consult yr own judgement as to the hour — in proposing nine or ten o'clock I imagined I was meeting yr principal objection. I see no mystery in it — as to any further proceeding about *you*, they have had enough of it, and Norton believes I have always continued to see you (according to Hockly.[2]). I neither wish to grieve or give trouble. You are welcome, if such be your wish, not to see me *"more than once"*, and to behave as if I were in the grave and out of your way after that. *I* have learned to sit alone, and *you* have learned to be happy & comfortable with others — so be it.

You were dining with Lady Stanhope & lounging & laughing, while I was undergoing my first evening *"out"* — & you can dine with her again after you have paid yr last visit to me.

This is the last trouble I shall give you & if you will let me know when, I will write to Ellice: pray decide, & it will be *over* for you as well as for me.

Caroline

Ellice said he would come at any time with you.

1. Edward Ellice (1781–1863), government whip in Grey's administration. A friend of both Caroline and Melbourne, Ellice on several occasions after the trial attempted to assist in patching up their relationship.

2. Possibly William Browne Hockley (1792–1860), who resided in India from 1813 until 1823, where he served as assistant to the chief secretary to the government of Bombay and later as criminal judge in Southern Concan. In 1821 Hockley was charged with acts of bribery and dismissed from his judgeship. After his return to England he published his memoirs and four other works, including *The English in India* (1828) in three volumes.

33

I am well enough to come down stairs today — and I am told that I over-rate the effect of these nervous attacks, which may continue thru ten years and I have been urged to "get out" — i.e. go into company.

You have not *asked* me for this intelligence — I give it therefore merely as a preface to what I have to say further. Before I begin to "go out" (which, in obedience to these excellent advisers, I mean to do next week) it is very requisite for my personal comfort that I should see you. I have two or three requests to make & explain, which I do not choose to write — which I never will attempt to get thru on paper — and which nevertheless I am anxious to urge.

It is part of the ridicule which is mixed with all the bitterness of my position that *I* am the one to propose & explain how you can pay a visit which another man — but that is not to the purpose.

I suppose your objection to be the dread of its being *known* — it is always after a pursuit has ceased to please that we weigh the risks. Now as there is no one but Sophia[1] & an old servant of my *grandfather's* in the house and as that old servant has already admitted Ellice two or three times when I have been drinking tea, nothing that I can see prevents *you* accompanying Ellice (unless you are afraid of *walking* from your house to mine) any evening that you can spare 1/2 an hour for that purpose.

124

I feel that I *have* a claim upon you, tho, like my claim to my children, there seems little willingness to admit it. I think it is not presuming very much on that claim, to propose you should pay *one* visit, even a little contre gré, considering that for some years I sate waiting, as my principal object, for your more *voluntary* calls. There is no woman *however strict*, who has not appeared to take it for granted I have seen you — most believe you came to Seymour's after the trial to "wish me joy" — great joy.

I *did* wish to see you any where — anyhow — perhaps even without being able to speak to you — anything to *see you again* — That is not at present my object. I will trouble you with no scene. I wish to say certain things to you — and you will pardon me, (since you speak somewhat bluntly yourself to *me*) — if I say that I have a right to expect to be heard: and that though you certainly have the *power* to add one other shade of irritation & mortified restlessness to the past, yet that it is the right of *might* you exert by refusal.

Since I have been ill, (that is for the most part ever since I came to town), my Uncle dines at the Clubs or with his friends — my evenings are spent invariably *alone* — Charles[2] not coming in till 2 in the morning. I cannot imagine who you expect will convict you of the heinous offence of seeing me again — or who has inspired you with so great a dread of the result, tho it is no doubt inspired for the best of purposes.

My Mother takes me tomorrow for two days to H.C.P.[3] imagining that *change* is good for me. If it is, God knows I have had enough & to spare of the remedy. I do not go till the evening if therefore you will send yr answer in the course of [the] morning, I would be glad. I cannot think you so utterly thankless & unfeeling, as to refuse what I repeat I ask as a grave favour & not out of sentiment or sorrow — and what *I* consider important, if indeed I am allowed to consider my own feelings of any importance whatever! It is my last request — or rather that

half hour will comprise all the requests I will ever make you —
and I hope those who have better fortune in their preference, will
be less troublesome.

Caroline

1. Mrs. Norton's maid.

2. Charles Sheridan. See above, Letter 29, n. 7 and Letter 8, n. 4.

3. Hampton Court Palace, begun in 1514 by Cardinal Wolsey and subsequently completed by Henry VIII. Mrs. Sheridan was given a private residence at Hampton Court shortly after her husband's death.

34

I am not much the better, but no matter.

God knows whether now or ever I desire to *suggest annoyances* to you, but that also is no matter now.

You know it is particularly offensive to me that Ellice should always be told of my letters to you. I am quite enough laughed at by men, without that — however he admitted there was no real obstacle, & that it was as easy as sending a note—

As you never explained or took the trouble to write on the subject, I do not see the objections as you do, because it is idle to tell *me* that such a visit is necessarily to be known. However be assured I will be the cause of no more annoyance to you. When I taxed you to find for me as much affection as, (if *you* had been the most crushed by what has occurred), *I* would have found for *you*, I required that which being involuntary is not commanded — when I asked you to pay that visit, it was with a view merely to certain points of advice & assistance — *that* required only a *voluntary effort, over a certain indolence & timidity;* and in refusing it you did *in fact* say "do not depend on me — make yr struggle as well as you can — I hope it will answer, but cannot interfere or attend to it."

You are afraid to visit me. I wish you had not been afraid also to tell me so *at first & from the first*. You shrink from *saying* painful things for the *rebound* of them upon yourself, and so we have moved uncertainly on, I not *understanding* what my position with you was to be, & you not choosing to say in clear

127

words, what however miserable it might make me, would at least have *decided* me & reversed many of the *negative* steps I have taken.

I think it is as well that this opportunity of explanation *has* come. I cannot regret it. What is simple "annoyance" to you, is balanced by agony for me, — and the uncontrollable restlessness is over. It is the worst blow, and I thank God it is the *last* that *can* come.

I am sorry to be nothing to you. I thought it would all come right again in time. I am sorry to be nothing, I had hoped to see more of you on to the end, but I had rather *know it*.

The only part of what I had to say which I can write, or which I can explain to the *intermediary* Ellice, is that I think while you talk of shielding *me* as well as yrself, you may as well speak to yr sister to fulfill the forms of society by calling & which I think is a *duty* on yr part under the circumstances[1] and when my family ask you to dinner &c you will go if you can (you need not be afraid of meeting *me* there — that will be taken care of —) as it is necessary for my reputation that the two families should *appear* to treat the whole thing as a vision & a lie.

Adieu what else I had to ask, is gone. I told you I *had* favours to ask. I have not received much encouragement to ask them. I hope that in time, the six years last past will fade from my memory, as they do more easily from yours, and I hope you will not find any other woman who is more willing to "suggest annoyances" — or more fiendish & diabolical in disposition—

I thought to the last that I might have depended on you — Adieu.

Yrs Caroline

1. Caroline Norton persistently requested that Melbourne persuade Lady Cowper to visit and to receive her. Lady Cowper, however, took an exceedingly dim view of her brother's association with Mrs. Norton, and she refused to become involved. Like most of his family, Melbourne's sister was more concerned with protecting his future than with assuaging Mrs. Norton's distress. Naturally Caroline was incensed by Lady Cowper's haughty fastidiousness, particularly as she was undoubtedly aware of the amatory relationship that lady enjoyed with Lord Palmerston for years before her first husband's death. In any case, relations between the two women eventually improved, and when Lord Palmerston died in November, 1865, Caroline addressed an affectionate letter to her former enemy: "It was my dream," she wrote, "when I thought to marry and live among the men who influenced their time, to be what I think you were, in this, the only reasonable ambition of woman . . . to have added so far to the happiness and security of a career of public usefulness and public elevation . . . " (Airlie, *Lady Palmerston*, 2: 180).

35

Thank you. I hope you do not think the worse of me. I hope not. I know it *is* the one thing in the world that is thought & felt to be contemptible & I well recollect the utter scorn I used to have for other women who did it, but I did not know then what it *was* to feel dependant [*sic*] on chances, to be obliged to consider all the future as a struggle & an insecurity. Remember my whole heart is bent on the power of transfering [*sic*] or leaving it to my boy: there is so much ill-feeling about him, so much wilful [*sic*] misconstruction that till I asked you this, I had nothing but bitterness thinking of him. I love them all dearly — I would have loved them all equally — but this link between him & me is that *I* only, love *him*.[1] If I feel that I shall not starve him by taking him, we will be together yet in spite of those who keep him just now. The only thing that grates me is what *you* think about it. I know you will *say* you think nothing of the request. I hope you will try &*feel* what you wd say from kindness — I was going to add "considering the peculiar circumstances," but every one thinks the peculiarity of *their* situation is their excuse.

I am very unwell today, because I am grown nervous & the hour of expectation yesterday made my heart beat — my head ache to say nothing of the evening after you were gone — but I am much the happier for having seen you — it makes the room seem more cheerful — it makes things seem less irrevocably wrecked round me. I hope I shall never write bitterly about yr people again, and I never intended to distrust your *word* given solemnly, but precisely in proportion to the trust felt in anyone, is the bitterness of the struggle of trying to compare *proofs & probabilities* with assertions made carelessly. I cannot understand it all, even now, and I still feel hurt & unhappy about some circumstances, the more because if you thought I was under the impression that you saw these people in the way you did, you must think my conduct as strange as yours seems to me. It is altogether a painful subject to me, more so than you imagine.

I do not wish to press upon you anything that you think you have reasons against, but I will not close my letter without saying that Uncle *volunteered* telling me he was sorry to see me grow more sad instead of better, & that if it was in his power by asking you to dine with us, or otherwise, to help me, he *would*.

I do not know how far he guessed that you accompanied Ellice — it was in the evening he spoke to me — he said it was *ridiculous* that our acquaintance should be at an end because of the past. Perhaps when the fine summer weather comes, & you are not obliged to drive such a short distance in your carriage you will think of it.

Brinsley[2] comes home on Tuesday. I hope you will be comfortable with him & my other people, and recollect on the other hand that tho' you cannot control the ill-will of some who dislike me, you *can* make the evidence of that ill-will less bitter to me, by not appearing to prefer their society to all the world.

Let them hate me & welcome — but do not let them hate me & *have you, too*. They *always* disliked me, but it did not always make me frantic — nor indeed give me a moments concern. It is *now*, that they seem to be *in my stead* that it stings me — and it is not true that all women hate each other — it is that one class & set of people who do.

God bless you — how well you are looking — better than last year — and I feel as if these few months had turned me into an old woman!

Yr Caroline

1. Her second son Brinsley was always Mrs. Norton's favorite. She grew particularly protective of him as a result of Norton's accusations about his paternity (see above, Letter 27) and her consequent suspicion that he especially suffered harsh treatment in the custody of Lady Menzies. In the interest of Brinsley's financial security, Caroline evidently sought and obtained from Melbourne either some measure of immediate monetary support or else the promise of a future legacy. Perhaps it was at this time that Melbourne determined to arrange for Caroline to receive a financial bequest at his death.

2. Mrs. Norton's elder brother.

36

16 Green St. Thursday [late Spring 1837]

I certainly did expect you would have written a line of some sort, if only to say whether you had spoken to your sister, and what she said. It seems as if you had forgotten all about me. I have been thinking of the other, viz Lady S.[tanhope] and I think you should say something to her.[1] We cut each other (or rather I cut her) from the mutual & instinctive conviction that we were at war on your account — *now* make her ask me, as she is, or imagines herself, the victor it will be all the easier. It is absurd to say you cant do it, for you have only so far to espouse my cause, as to stay away [from] two or three parties yourself if it is not done. If this seems utterly out of the question, then great indeed must your preference be, since you would rather *wound me* than run even a remote risk of *teasing her.* I do not & cannot see the justice or good feeling of your being with her, if she chooses to run counter to me. I dont want you to say in so many words "if you dont ask Mrs. N.[orton] I shant come" — like a proud school-boy, but I *do* think you should mention it & then tacitly shew your opinion. These sort of things are all the service you can ever render me for much past discomfort & I think if you cannot bring yourself to make even *that* exertion with your immediate associates, you certainly cannot talk of shewing me kindness or friendship.

Your not writing all these days, is no great sign of anything of the sort. I hope you did not come here to mock me.

The last agreeable feature of my life is a threatening letter from Trelawny.[2] I told him in the civilest way possible that he must discontinue his visits now that I was awkwardly situated, and that his name had been used by N.[orton] amongst others. I paid him every species of compliment in the course of the few sentences I spoke, tho' I spoke decidedly. He went into the rage of a savage — so much so that he couldnt speak in reply, and *wrote* his answer in the style of the Arabian Nights mixed up with his own novel of "The Younger Son"[3] — mysteriously awful, & vaguely sublime, but very fierce. He did not vouchsafe to say what he would do, but great things are to be done: and I am to be "a *skiff*

> Day & night & night & day
> Drifting on its dreary way

without rudder, compass, or pilot," & finally I am to be "a *hulk*", an ungraceful end, but it is my doom. I did a sensible thing when I made his acquaintance! However his note gave me the first *defying* moment I have had. I have been so sorrowful or so wild about all my misery, but when I read this effusion there crept over me the sort of dogged & contemptuous resistance N's personal violence used to inspire. I believe I shall end by hating every one & distrusting every one — I, that set out by believing & liking all who did not openly & manifestly oppose me.

I think your not writing most unkind. Mr. N. has admitted to Marryat[4] yesterday *his total disbelief of the charges against you, & the consequent injustice of the trial* — but he says, I wished to marry *another* man (name not given) & *therefore* he keeps the children. I think this looks like a step — an opening for me. I am considering of this vague "man", and will conquer the shadow & see N. myself. I will not write you the whole story tho it wd amuse you, about Marryats interview. You are so coldly careless that it is superfluous trouble for you.

Yrs Caroline

1. Caroline continued to beseech Melbourne to have Lady Cowper and Lady Stanhope receive her at their respective homes, but her petitions came to nothing.

2. Edward John Trelawny (1792–1881), author, soldier of fortune, and adventurer-friend of Byron and Shelley. In the company of Byron, Trelawny acted as pagan priest at Shelley's cremation on the shore of the Gulf of Spezia, and he rescued the poet's heart from the pyre and preserved it. Later he published his *Recollections of the Last Days of Shelley and Byron* (1858). Trelawny showed marked interest in Mary Shelley after her husband's death and subsequently in Mrs. Norton, whose home he frequented in the early 1830s and for whom he had a vast admiration. In a May, 1836, letter to Claire Clairmont, Mary Shelley's step-sister, in which he set down his opinions about the Nortons' marital discord and the impending trial, Trelawny referred to Caroline as "the Lady of song and beauty" and "the divine Mrs. Norton" and labeled her husband a fool "as gross as ignorance made drunk" (Trelawny, *Letters of Edward John Trelawny,* pp. 199–201. In describing George Norton, Trelawny made use of two lines from a speech of Iago's in Shakespeare's *Othello,* III. iii. 404–5).

3. The autobiographical work from which, before its publication in 1831, Mary Shelley persuaded Trelawny to delete certain objectionable passages relating to her husband.

4. Frederick Marryat (1792–1848), a captain in the Royal Navy and the author of a series of novels about sea life, including *Peter Simple* (1834) and *Mr. Midshipman Easy* (1836). Marryat edited the *Metropolitan Magazine* from 1832 until 1835.

I N MID-MAY Caroline visited her husband at his lodgings in Wilton Place, where he broke down completely, admitted that he had never really believed her guilty of the "last offence," and begged her to come back to him. He promised the immediate return of the children from Scotland and proposed that they set up house at the country estate left him by Miss Vaughan. Remarkably, Norton's rancor seemed entirely placated, and he actually spoke to his wife with reason and affection. Caroline was exhausted, and she feared that she might never regain her boys while she lived apart from him. Miserable in the confused and degraded position of a separated wife, she was, as she later expressed it, "willing to make a raft out of the wreck, and so drift back," even to what had heretofore been "a comfortless haven."[1] In short, she agreed to return to her husband.

Norton's family intervened again, however, and within a fortnight Caroline was informed that it would not be possible just yet for the children to leave Rannoch Lodge. In the meantime Norton suggested that she go to Scotland herself or perhaps visit Lord Grantley at Wonersh and attempt to win his compliance. On May 30 Caroline replied in a letter which recounted Norton's various proposals and indicted his brutal inconsistencies and his spiritless subservience to Grantley and his other implacably hostile relatives. Norton was evidently not impervious to his wife's charges; and, though he again suggested the necessity of several monetary concessions from Caroline, he soon arranged his sons' departure from Scotland. They arrived in England on June 10, and on the 13th Norton sent them to Green Street to spend the day with their mother.

1. Perkins, *Mrs. Norton,* p. 117

37

[16 Green Street] June 3d [1837]

The flowers were yours? I saw the familiar face of one of the pale carnations, and it was like meeting an old companion after years & events — one of the *glad-sorrows* of life. It is a long time since I had any from you. I am glad that they are the first flowers I have had this year from *any one* — glad to be thought of — glad to see anything that looked so like old happy days — notwithstanding that I could not put them in the vases without sitting down to cry.

I expect the boys on the 7th, but there may be another weeks delay.

God bless you.

Caroline

June 3ᵈ

The flowers were yours? I saw the familiar face of one of the pale carnations, and it was like meeting an old companion after years & events — one of the glad-sorrows of life. it is a long long time since I had any from you — & I am glad that they are the first flowers I have had this year from any one — glad the thought of — glad to see anything that looked so like old happy days — notwithstanding that I could not put them in the vases without sitting down to cry.

I expect the boys on the 7ᵗʰ, but there may be another weeks delay.

God bless you   Caroline

38

Wednesday [*16 Green Street, June 7, 1837*]

God forbid that with all drawbacks included, I should not feel *most thankful* at the prospect of having my children with me again: but I wait to feel glad till they are really here. You have no conception of the shuffling, the tyranny, the cunning, with which I have to contend — and it would put *lead* even into *your* heart to perceive in every line of the letters I receive, how completely *money* is the avowed object of our attempted "reconciliation." I hold a letter of this morning in which there is this sentence: *"I do wish* (apros-pos of debts) *you would tell me what you are prepared to do if you have your boys sent to you."* A man can hardly say in plainer words, "what will you *bid* for your children, if I sell my right to keep them from you?"

He mixes up with the sentences about them, descriptions of his furniture, & calculations of what it costs. He asked me the day I saw him if *I* had any furniture to contribute. I made a sort of bitter answer, asking whether he had sent for me as Greenacre sent for Mrs Brown, to ascertain her property; & ever since, he has been so enchanted with the comparison that he does nothing but sign himself, *your affectionate Intended, Greenacre.*[1]

My conviction is, that he is *insane*. A year or two more, & perhaps other people will also perceive it.

We are very glad about Bridgewater[2] which we hope will fall yet to Brinsley's share. Frank[3] has been over for four days very much improved, & eager about *grave* things. All this occupies me. I am better but very nervous. How are *you?*

140

God bless you — thank you for your last note — it was more *comfortable* to me than lately. I believe you have often done things both to please and vex me, without knowing the full extent of either effect, and your flowers were among the *random* shots which flew on the pleasant side.

Yours ever
Caroline

1. The allusion is to James Greenacre, who murdered his prospective fifth wife on Christmas Eve, 1836, and was subsequently hanged. His victim, a washerwoman named Hannah Brown, had been persuaded to bring her property to Greenacre's house under the pretext of marriage. Caroline humored Norton in his bizarre jest, and for some time he addressed her as Mrs. Brown and referred to himself as Greenacre.

2. Evidently some portion of the Sheridan family property.

3. Frank Sheridan, Caroline Norton's brother. See above, Letter 3, n. 6.

39

Thursday [16 Green Street, June 15, 1837]

Many thanks for the flowers. They came just after the children were seated round me, & but for being hurried & heavy hearted, I would have written before to thank you.

We have so little communication, & it is so *impossible* to write all details of affairs as tediously progressive as mine, that I will only say the boys are here in London, & he promises they shall come every day — but there is such shuffling & changing & such an evident desire to outwit me & get *me* nailed about *money*, & leave all besides at his own will & pleasure, that I do not yet feel assured or comfortable about them.

They are looking tolerably well, with the exception of Brin, who is grown more nervous than before, is a perfect skeleton, and appears to me to be growing crooked; I am to shew him to Brodie[1] tomorrow. He is very merry all the same. The little one is the sharpest little fellow you ever saw, & speaks as fluently as I do. They were very happy at returning, but cannot understand going away in the evening.[2]

The eldest & youngest have purses full of sixpences, and talked of little else for two hours. Brin's private fortune I have not yet heard mentioned, so I am in great hopes I have one son who does not resemble his Father, in thinking money *the* object of life.

I have no more to say except that I feel very sad, and still miss *a child*, for this sharp talkative little being, does not seem to me my fat fair baby. They grow up in such a moment!

Adieu — if you will tell the woman[3] who now gets your

142

personal news to forward your notes for perusal, I will be glad. I hear nothing of you as I used to do, and feel much the same dreariness of heart that one does when watching by a sick bed: — every thing very cold, very dim, & very silent, & the clock ticking very loud.

Yrs Caroline

1. Sir Benjamin Brodie (1783–1862), the famous surgeon who attended George IV and later served as sergeant-general to both William IV and Queen Victoria. Brodie was created a baronet in 1834, and in 1858 he was elected president of the Royal Society.

2. During the week the Norton children were in London, they spent each day with their mother but returned to their father at 10 Wilton Place at night.

3. Presumably Lady Stanhope, Caroline's particular *bête noire*.

HAVING ACHIEVED A DEGREE OF SERENITY in her relations with Melbourne, Caroline Norton was more content during the autumn and winter of 1837–38 than she had been since before the trial. She wrote with renewed vitality, dashing off drafts of her poems to John Murray, who in exchange sent her a variety of books and periodicals. In November she received and read *Don Juan*. Subsequently she wrote to Murray that though she admired the wit and originality of Byron's comic epic, she found it excessively jaunty and irreverent, less pleasing than his romances, which she dearly loved. The effect of *Don Juan*, she wrote, "is like hearing some sweet and touching melody familiar to me . . . suddenly struck up in quick time with all the words parodied."[1]

All the while Caroline continued her efforts to gain control of her children. Norton eventually expressed a wish for the appointment by either side of referees who would attempt to untangle the complicated negotiations and settle the questions of custody and allowance once and for all. Caroline named Serjeant Talfourd and Norton chose John Bayley, a fairminded man who, during the course of several months, worked diligently at finding some kind of terms agreeable to both husband and wife. Bayley made several proposals, to each of which Caroline consented, but every time a solution seemed in sight, Norton altered his demands. At last Bayley quarreled with his unscrupulous client, dissolved their association, and sent an entirely sympathetic letter to Caroline in which he expressed his "unbounded contempt" for her husband's petty duplicities and his unreasonable requirements. "If the devil is not in him," Bayley declared of Norton, "there is no such spirit. . . . I blush for human nature when I see a woman so cruelly treated by a man, and that man her husband!"[2]

Caroline attended many of the parties celebrating the queen's coronation in the summer of 1838, but she was not accepted at court. Her *amour-propre* demanded that she receive this official recognition of respectability, and without Melbourne's support she could not hope to do so. The queen was exceedingly sensitive about reputation, and indeed she was reluctant to receive, and thus tacitly approve, anyone to whom the slightest taint attached. Consequently, Melbourne refused to propose an invitation for Caroline, and he thereby again incurred her exasperated indignation. Soon she was writing more bitter letters decrying the arrestment of his friendship and his loyalty. By the end of the year all her latent resentment at being shut out of his life and her jealousy of his female acquaintance had come vigorously back to life.

1. Perkins, *Mrs. Norton*, pp. 117–18.
2. Acland, *Caroline Norton*, p. 118.

40

The daughter[1] may be yours for anything I know — I dare say is, by the enthusiastic defence — the man whose abuse of this woman I *believed,* is *yrself,* for *you* told me she swore false on the sacrament, & that she told you so herself;[2] also that she was Frederics mistress instead of yours — and *I* have her poetical letter to you, in which she describes herself "watering her geraniums thinking of *you*[["]] — as also some of yours about her — which if I had had the "boa constrictor wisdom" she and you think I need, events have taught me how much truth there was in yr denials — before I lost my boys that you might then swear in court you were nothing to me —

I see nothing more "fiendish & diabolical" in *my* injuring those women than in *their* injuring me, who never offended them — yr romantic affection for them makes *their* injury to me no fault — be it so. Like all other experiences mine comes a little to[o] late to serve me. I leave to you and Lady Stanhope the satisfaction, such as it is, of duping & baffling one very easily duped — and to whom you[r] best & most continual taunt is that she *believed* you! I "knew you *saw* these women" — yes — you forget *my* idea of seeing people is not to see them all on the same terms. I think if yr preference for Lady Stanhope was so very decided it is a pity you made such a useless needless wreck of my life, when you *had* a woman whose husband is quite contented it should be so — a liaison which suits yr sister & your people much better than I. However there she is — make the most of her — credulity lasts a long time but it does not *come back again*. You need not taunt me with my *knowledge* of yr intimacy, for it was never proved to me till very lately — and now that it *is* proved you have a hold over *one* — not over *both* as you had.

As to what I am "capable of" — you have seen what folly I am capable of for the sake of a preference — what I am capable of besides, you have to learn. I deserved that you should have played *true* — you have not done it — and you are the last human being who has any *right* to judge actions whose spring of evil rests with yrself & never shewed till you woke it.

I wish you happy with Lady Stanhope — she suits you. You are of a nature to be contented under the circumstances — & I hope that I shall become so.

[a flourish, but no signature]

1. The reference is apparently to Lady Stanhope's only daughter, Catherine Lucy Wilhelmina Stanhope (1819–1901), who married Lord Dalmeny in 1843 and in 1854, three years after her first husband's death, wed the fourth duke of Cleveland. A celebrated beauty, particularly as a young girl, she was remembered by the duke of Argyll as "the prettiest woman . . . after the Duchess of Sutherland" in all the company of ladies (mostly peeresses and their daughters) whom he had ever observed at the queen's annual openings of Parliament (George Douglas, *George Douglas, Eighth Duke of Argyll: Autobiography and Memoirs,* ed. the Dowager Duchess of Argyll, 1: 150).

2. I have found no information regarding this supposed false swearing of Lady Stanhope's.

41

I congratulate you on your influence at the palace. There is Lady Stanhope whose husband deals abuse out to you all, & is a "rank" Tory dining for the second time at the Palace since I have been in town, while Seymour's wife[1] (Seymour being not only your own supporter but holding a government situation) has been considered all this year not good enough company for Royalty & its attendants — Here is a little family reunion of you, the Queen, & the woman you never made a doubt has been yr brother's mistress, (if she hasn't also been yours), — who swore a lie on the Sacrament, & lives exactly as she pleases; — whose rank, whose conduct, whose position in no way entitle her to any consideration, such as is by your means lavished upon her — whom every one mentions as your mistress & wonders at your thrusting her on the Queen (of course you dont believe it) here she is, put above Georgiana whose conduct no one can cavil at, & who has married the heir to the second dukedom in the Kingdom. You probably think from hearing nothing of it, that Seymour takes it quietly — perhaps you will be more enlightened by & by. The last time I spoke of this you told me that you had no hand in the invitation, but you imagined it was thought agreeable to you. Taking this as the exact fact what does it prove? Why, that while you contrive to give the impression civil[it]y to Lady Stanhope is *agreeable to you* you must contrive also to give the impression that civility or kindness to those who belong to *me* is a matter of indifference, as indeed the result of my petition & the insolent overlooking of the Seymours has proved.

If you think I will bear it all for ever, you are mistaken. I have been blind — wilfully blind — I have not believed what you chose to contradict — scarcely my own observation — but I will not be the only one to suffer — I will proclaim what this woman is, who is so fortunately protected & who [tries?] without observation the visits to you which in me were *crime*. I presume even in her case scarcely proper — let her try to disprove it & many other small irregularities your own servants can testify to.

You have treated me with the most selfish ingratitude — you have left nothing either to hope or to fear — your hold over me never was fear of consequences, but a personal feeling, which it has been yr good pleasure to insult and destroy. We will see whether under the *mask* of justice, I shall be told by the Queen that I am not fit to associate with the ladies of her court, while she makes a companion of one whom your "guardianship of Royalty" does not consider an unfit associate.[2] There are few trodden on in this world who do not sting in return — & if ever there was one who struggled to the last *not* to resent *injury*, the most open neglect, & opposition it has been me — tho you may sneer at the assertion because you know nothing of what has been felt thought or struggled with & probably think a few angry words on paper to you is enough & more than enough for all—

Will God help me for I am very miserable.

1. Georgiana, Lady Seymour, Caroline Norton's sister. (See above, Letter 1, n. 1.)
2. Mrs. Norton's abiding resentment and disapproval of Queen Victoria, no doubt largely initiated by the queen's rebuff of both herself and members of her

family, is reflected in her comments to Edward Robert Lytton (later first earl of Lytton) in a letter written shortly after the publication in 1868 of Queen Victoria's *Journal of Our Life in the Highlands:*

> I think of writing a pamphlet "Common Sense on the Queen's Book" saying the truth, pro & con, instead of the nonsense of compliment the papers have held to — as a Review of that piece of Royal Authorship.
>
> There is something in the blind selfishness of her clamorous sorrow, — that never seems to have *noticed* grief, till it came in a Court dress & was presented to her, — that is truly marvellous! As is this notion of her *meritorious* conduct in loving a handsome young Prince whom she had desired to marry.
>
> Did no young couple ever love & agree before?
>
> Were none ever parted by Death before?
>
> Ld Melbourne was a wise old man & he *prophecied* that if ever she survived Albert, her wilfulness "would break out in some act of great folly." errata — read acts *in the plural.*

(This undated letter is located among the Lytton papers in the Hertford County Record Office; the extract above is quoted with the kind consent of Lady Hermione Cobbold.)

42

You have a great deal to read, but first I tell you that I have sent to your house 2 doz. claret glasses — They were ordered last year, before I knew we were to be such very *distant* acquaintances — and as they were finished I send them for yr birthday, with a sulky heart, because of the dinners *you will* give to other people — and I did not like to add *your* birthday to the many blank anniversarys I have had to keep this year & the last.

I saw Norton on Saturday at his office — in the private room; by the aidance & abetting of Mr. Hardwick.[2] It would be *very* long to tell you *all* he said, for I staid nearly 3 hours; the only *distinct points* were that he denied having been in any way responsible for the trial — that he said his love & sympathy were so great for me, that he would certainly have challenged you if you had not married me — & that his principal objection to giving me the boys was the dread of opposing God, who had made him the humble instrument of sobering one of the lightest & most thoughtless hearts in the world, which he trusted grief & disappointment would eventually bring round to the Throne of Grace. He said he would send the children to me if I would take a female companion of his choosing named Miss Cole. (I knew her at school). But upon my ready acquiescence, he backed out of his proposal & said, that on account of his family, he wd prefer sending the children to Miss Cole & putting me on equal terms with himself as to seeing them — (as a *beginning*) & that afterwards they might come to me. This also I acquiesced in, &

it was agreed he shd see Brinsley but Brin. made the excuse of being obliged to leave town: which I wrote as politely as I could, to N.[orton]. I enclose his note in consequence, & my reply which being dated today, is the present predicament of our affairs. In any other human being his note & his conduct would go for nothing — but with him it shows that his *other* mood is coming on & I am sanguine that some settlement will be come to, about the boys, & that soon.

I think I did not over-rate my own influence, as *face to face*, for I assure you, before I went, I began to fear, his *conditions* would be that I should give him a lift in the carriage & come home again. *He* defended himself to *me*, point by point — and could not even *act* the part of an outraged husband: which acting would indeed have been superfluous after my *opening speech*, which was, "*I am here to speak about my children — & I am here because I feel that the conviction is wanting in your mind which wd make this meeting an indecency & a ridicule for both of us.*" He asked me to take a chair — called me "poor dear Cary" — & was as quiet as possible. I wish I could say as *rational* — but any one more utterly insane I never talked to except Lady Kirkwall![3]

I have been so much interrupted since I began this, that I will close it now. I could have wished you to have called today at any time — you would not do it — & the not seeing you at all — makes my letter writing seem heavy to me.

The Sefton people[4] are very impertinent to me — but being crooked & old maids it is not to be marvelled at. . . . Lady Stanhope & her daughter[5] do their "possible" to be rude, but having a good profile I invariably looked over the crowd. Mrs. Fox Lane talked with an air of patronage, which I returned with a grateful smile — Poodle Byng thinks he could easily find me some other occupation — & Lady Albro'[6] [*sic*] has written me down for her young *men & women* dinners.

Good-bye — I dare say it has never occurred to you that this is a day I used always to contrive to see you — it makes the day bitter to me — but I hope there will never be anything to make it unwelcome to you — God bless you—

Caroline

1. Melbourne's sixtieth birthday.

2. John Hardwick (1791–1875), a barrister and colleague of George Norton's. He was appointed magistrate at Lambeth in 1821 and later at Marlborough Street, where he served from 1841 until 1856. When the Norton children came to London during the Christmas holidays of 1841, Hardwick supervised their interviews with Caroline. He incurred Norton's extreme displeasure by permitting Caroline one evening to accompany her children to a play, thus allowing the mother and sons to be seen alone together in public.

3. Born Anna Maria De Blaquiere, Lady Kirkwall (d. 1843) was the widow of John Fitz-Maurice, viscount Kirkwall (1778–1820).

4. The family of Charles William Molyneux, third earl of Sefton (1796–1855), M.P. for South Lancaster, 1832–34, and lord lieutenant of Lancaster from 1851 until his death.

5. See above, Letter 40, n. 1.

6. Lady Aldborough, the former Mary Arundell, second wife of Mason Gerard Stratford, fifth earl of Aldborough (1784–1849).

43

*Rome.*¹ *Thursday December 19th* [*1839*]

Thank you. I got your letter and the enclosure — and thought all you said very kind; and am not touchy about your good nature about my staying abroad: I ought to have answered it immediately, but your second short letter did not reach me for a day or two because you made the N. of my name in that erring & shortsighted manner which deceives foreign postmasters into claiming my letters for some imaginary Mrs. Horton, and which only my frenzied activity ever obtains out of their box.

I leave Rome tomorrow morning at nine. I had already left it, but having been overturned & the carriage broken in pieces, I was obliged to return, and put off the journey for a couple of days to buy another, which we have done with tolerable success, finding an Englishman anxious to give up his. I was not much hurt, but a good deal shook & frightened, and my head has ached ever since with the knock it received. It is lucky this, our only accident, did not happen on the Corniche road, for most assuredly you would have no more letters in the crabbed little hand writing you have been so long accustomed to. I do not wish to stay longer abroad this year, tho' I hope to come again, and have learnt & seen more in these six weeks than in the six last years. I cannot feel quiet till I have tried my last about my children and I have also bad news from my poor Mother, who has lost the sight of one eye and the other going from cataract. Helen seems very low indeed about her & I should like to be back and with them to see how she gets on. It is a sad thing & makes me very *unhappy*, tho' Travers² is sanguine about the success of the operation he proposes to try when the proper time arrives. Poor little Mother; she led such a busy occupied life, and read so much and did so much for other people, that it falls heavily on her.

Marcia Sheridan[3] has another child and I am to be god mother. It seems to me only yesterday the other was born — there are not above eleven months between the two last — & Brinsley is now the respectable Father of three children. They are in Paris, so I shall see them as I go through. Rome is a place in which if it were ever possible to feel independent of society & its ways it would be more easy to do so than in any other — but in spite of my love for painting sculpture & antiquities, — in spite of the dayly occupations of the most agreeable and instructive sort which I have enjoyed, — I cannot help being glad, or rather feeling *relieved* at going away, when I consider the coldness of the few English, & the puzzled curiosity of the foreigners as to my position. I have not had one friend here the whole time — I have met just enough acquaintances to enable strangers to judge how it was the fashion to treat me in England, and act accordingly. What I have said to you before is most just & true, that I am worse off than another woman might be, because my name, my family, & something in myself, makes me an object of attention & curiosity — and turns all that was a flattery into insult. You have thought me irritable about the Court & all that business. I think it is enough to make one irritable to see what the caprice of a sick old King may inflict, and the want of help from those who might have helped me. It is [nothing?] to the Queen or to you that I should not be able to command the [company?] of one female companion while I have been here — but it is something to *me* when I come in after my sightseeing is over and sit down by the fireside in my hotel, to feel that wherever I go, this shadow walks after me.

I am afraid this will be a dull letter for you to get from so great a distance but I am out of spirits. Write me a line to Paris for I shall come home now, and shall probably be a week with Brinsley and his wife there. I heard an account of Lord Winchelsea[4] [*sic*] which would have amused you; while he was

155

at [illegible]. First, being eager to see all that was to be seen, he went about on a donkey, which tho' a respectable & strong animal when drawing a costermonger's cart, is considered weak & undignified as the *montûre* of a fat British Peer. Well, he heard that there was a man who could whistle down the chamois-goat, and his soul was fired with the notion of being a chamois hunter; so he set out with another English nobleman, donkey & all; & the guide whistled & climbed, & climbed & whistled, and Winchelsea & his donkey panted & toiled up the steep ascents, one after the other, but no chamois appeared. At last the noble Lord turned to his companion and says he, "Gad, I dont like this at all — I wont climb any further — Gad, I believe the fellow's laughing at us; hoaxing us; Gad I've a mind *to get off & lick him*." The unconscious chamois hunter continued to whistle, & the friend to dissuade Winchelsea from these martial intentions; they returned without seeing any sport — and the whole evening he murmured to himself as he dozed in his chair, "Gad, I wish I'd licked that fellow; if ever I meet that fellow again I'll lick him." I heard another story of him that made me laugh — it seems he is a most restless & energetic man, and every now & then, when things are going wrong in other people's affairs, or something is done which he disapproves of, he says, "The time was now come when I felt myself called upon to interfere" — tho *why* he felt himself called on to interfere does not clearly appear. Now old Lord Brudenell[5] had a mistress, and as the mistress, or he himself, wished to do the thing decently, she lived in a neighboring village and he rode to see her in a white great coat, & pretended he was a doctor but he was at last found out, in consequence of one of the villagers wanting a child prescribed for, and he could never ride thro again without being mobbed and every one shouting out "the doctor." In short, there was much scandal and Lord Winchelsea thought "the time was come for *him* to interfere," so he sits down & writes a long letter of rebuke to Ld Brudenell — "But," says the friend to whom he told the story, "upon what grounds my dear Lord — did you — you understand—" "Why["] says Lord W. ["]upon

156

the grounds of my being *magistrate in the county*, I told him I couldn't suffer such a thing in the county; that I felt myself *called upon* to interfere; and the fellow wrote me such a violent letter in reply as would astonish you." I can't tell you how delighted I am with these accounts of him & there are more, but too long for a letter. The only other amusing thing here is my Uncles conduct relative to a certain dish composed of stewed wild-boar, or *ciniali*, as they call it, — which dish he is so passionately fond of, that he is never easy till he has ascertained whether it is to appear at dinner. Now a French or Italian hotel being a scrambling large place with an open court, he saunters down & asks any one he sees, this mysterious question — "Do *you* know if there is *Ciniali* today?" But as he is both blind & inattentive, he does not secure the cook or waiter to answer him, but sometimes a mercer coming to shew brocades to some fine lady in the hotel, sometimes a strange courier, sometimes a dapper little Italian Count who is leaving his card as a valued visitor, sometimes a hired coachman waiting for orders — and you have no idea what absurd mistakes & contretemps have arisen out of this. As to the Vatican, Colosseum, statues, pictures, — he has a horror of them, & yawns & groans all the time he is there. My doctor said he had known ladies seized with convulsive sickness from over exertion & sightseeing in Rome upon which Charles Sheridan declared he did not wonder at it, & felt something of the same sort himself. I saw in a shop of curiosities & pictures the other day, a small black cabinet inlaid with ivory etchings, of birds, & in the centre, (to my astonishment) your favorite subject of a woman whipping a child, (or a nymph whipping Bacchus, or some such thing, for I was not alone, & could not inspect it). I had half a mind to buy it for you, but thought the difficulty of carrying a bad contraband *joke* to England & perhaps having it seized at the Custom house ought to deter me. Nor was it pretty in any way. I am sorry to say the Italian women appear utterly to neglect this important branch of education as far as their children are concerned — but in these warm relaxing sirocco winds nobody does *anything*: and indeed

157

I am told that during their prevalence all the Italians consider themselves so utterly inadequate to exertion, that they retire even from the nuptial chamber and leave their ladies to the charitable exertions of such young Englishmen as may yet have resisted the Italian climate.

The Jew's Quarter here is a very curious thing. I was in it the other day, looking at old brocades & damasks, which may be had very cheap. It strikes me as rather an anomaly that we Christian Protestants should only be allowed a place of worship outside the gates of Rome, & that these Crucifiers should live in the heart of the Eternal City. But there they are — cheating, slop-selling, & rag-mending; the Ishmaels of the earth wherever they go, but looking to the day when they shall once more be a nation, and, I suspect, secretly despising us, even more than we look down on them. God bless you. My head aches dreadfully, but I wished to write to you before I started again (I hope more prosperously) from Rome. I trust the Queen's marriage[6] may prove advantageous in all ways & to all concerned. It seems so odd the little interest taken here, about England or its Sovereign. Let me hope Jack Frost is hung.[7] God forgive me for jesting on any man's life. Take care of yourself — dont do imprudent things as to health, and think of me a little. I will write again from Florence in four or five days.

Ever yours
Car.

1. In October, 1839, Caroline and her uncle Charles Sheridan went to southern Italy in the company of her sister and brother-in-law, Helen and Price Dufferin (fourth baron Dufferin and Claneboye). Apparently the Dufferins were on holiday only a short time, but Caroline and her uncle remained in Italy until early January, when they returned to London and took up residence at 24 Bolton Street.

2. Benjamin Travers (1783–1858). the eye surgeon. Travers became president of the Royal Medical and Chiurgical Society in 1827. and in 1837 he was made surgeon extraordinary to Queen Victoria.

3. Mrs. Richard Brinsley Sheridan. Caroline's sister-in-law.

4. George William Finch-Hatton. ninth earl of Winchilsea and fifth earl of Nottingham (1791–1858). a violent opponent of Catholic relief, the 1832 Reform Bill. and other liberal measures. His vehement opposition to the 1829 Catholic Relief Bill led to a duel with the duke of Wellington. whom Winchilsea accused of "an insidious design" for the infringement of English liberties and for "the introduction of popery into every department of the state" (see the *Dictionary of National Biography, sub* Finch-Hatton). The meeting took place in Battersea Fields on March 21. 1829. The duke fired his weapon and missed. whereupon Winchilsea fired in the air and then apologized for his intemperate language.

5. Robert Brudenell. sixth earl of Cardigan (1769–1837). M.P. for Marlborough from 1797 until 1802; father of the seventh earl of Cardigan, who distinguished himself at Balaklava when he led the Light Brigade to glory and destruction.

6. Queen Victoria. betrothed on October 15. 1839. was married on February 10. 1840.

7. John Frost. chartist and leader of an armed mob that in 1839 rose up at Newport in "Jack Frost's Revolt." Frost was not hanged but was instead transported to Van Dieman's Land (Tasmania) in 1840 and was later pardoned.

44

Georgiana says, and says very justly, that as, owing to her being so very seldom asked to the Palace to dinner, she has very little opportunity of seeing Mme. Lehzen[1] and as, if she commits herself & me by requesting a private interview, she may be told by the Baroness, very politely, that she "would be *so glad*, but has *no influence over the Queen!*" — she wishes to know, from you, whether there are any grounds for supposing such would *not* be her reception, & how it would be best to set about the business as regards the baroness herself.

You have taken this very coldly & very lightly — that is your own affair — and "*you* are *you*" — as Ld Normanby[2] is good enough to write to me — but let this terminate unfavorably, and if I do not give your "pleasant friends" something to talk of with you at your Palace *family dinners*, — more distinct & less allegorical than your Wife's Princess of Madagascar & *her* court,[3] believe for the future in women *liking* mortification. To *them* at least I do not owe even the *memory* of regard. I understand trampling on Lady Flora Hastings[4] is found more difficult than trampling on me: and I have no doubt the demands made by her friends or relatives are not so easily put by, *even by you*, as mine are — me to whom you have no scruple in first promising you will do a thing, then giving a reason for the delay, & then saying you wont do it at all! Why did you *say* you would give this accursed book if you did not mean it? Why are you not frank at once, instead of shuffling even in your unkindness? It does not seem so *difficult* to refuse me, but what you might save me at least the uncertainty — but that is over — over for ever. I dare say you look back with a light & unreproaching heart not only to the ruin of *my* destiny, but to others which in a different degree depended on you — it is the better for you, & there is "the blue sky bending over all":[5] — (to which sky the children look, believing God sits *there* to judge the earth[)].

1. Formerly the Princess Victoria's governess, the baroness Lehzen remained an influential figure at court until she returned to Germany in 1842.

2. Sir Constantine Henry Phipps, first marquess of Normanby and second earl of Mulgrave (1797–1863); governor of Jamaica from 1832 until 1834, when he became lord privy seal, with a seat in the cabinet, under Melbourne. In 1835 Normanby was sent to Ireland as lord-lieutenant, and in 1839 he was appointed secretary of war and the colonies.

3. In her novel *Glenarvon* (1816), Lady Caroline Lamb satirized the redoubtable Lady Holland, who was something of a social tryant, as the "Princess of Madagascar" (see Clarke Olney, *"Glenarvon* Revisited," pp. 271–76).

4. Lady Flora Hastings (1806–39), daughter of Frances Rawdon, first marquess of Hastings, and maid of honour to the duchess of Kent. In the early months of 1839 Queen Victoria became convinced, on very little evidence, that Lady Flora was pregnant by the queen's archenemy, Sir John Conroy. Moralist that she was, Victoria would not rest until she had exposed her mother's maid of honour. Melbourne characteristically advised the queen to do nothing for a time, but the queen rejected his counsel to delay and persuaded him to have Lady Flora examined by the court physician, Sir James Clarke. Lady Flora did not in fact prove to be pregnant, her family was naturally outraged by the insult, and the whole affair damaged the public image of both the queen and her prime minister.

5. Samuel Taylor Coleridge, "Christabel," part I, 1. 331: "For the blue sky bends over all!"

SOON AFTER HER RETURN FROM ITALY, in January, 1840, Caroline once again renewed the struggle for her children. With the passing of the Infant Custody Bill the previous summer, she felt she had more bargaining leverage than before. She delayed applying to the lord chancellor, hoping that her husband might capitulate in order to avoid legal action, but he proved as obstinate and uncooperative as ever. When Caroline wrote to Norton about access, he replied that he could not yet permit the children to return to England, and to neutralize her disappointment, he offered to send her recent portraits of their sons. "If you knew what affection was," Caroline responded in early March, "you would feel what a mockery it must seem to be denied the children themselves, not even to be allowed to correspond with them, and then be offered their pictures! . . . I, on my part, wonder you can look in the children's faces, or at their pictures either, and not feel ashamed and reproached by the memory of the unmanly persecution which has pursued their mother through four dogged, unrelenting years!"[1]

All through the summer and autumn of 1840 Caroline lived in expectation of her husband's submission to her wishes. He tentatively promised to have Sir Neil Menzies send the boys to London, and Caroline waited, more patiently than in the past, comforted by the thought that if all else failed, she now had legal recourse. During the latter part of the year, however, her hopes suffered another bitter reversal, when she discovered that the English Court had no authority over children residing in Scotland.

In the summer of 1841 the boys were sent to an English school. Caroline again threatened to petition the lord chancellor, and Norton grudgingly yielded her visiting privileges at the school and permitted her to see the children during the Christmas holidays. But it was not until the following autumn, when a mutual bereavement obliged a kinder spirit in her husband, that she had access to any of her children on the terms she desired. In September, 1842, while the three boys were with their father at Kettlethorpe, William, the youngest, was thrown from his pony. He suffered a scratch on his arm, which was neglected, and within a fortnight he was dead of blood poisoning. Thereafter Norton gave up all opposition to Caroline's right to unobstructed access to Fletcher and Brinsley. The next decade saw little recrudescence of her husband's antagonism, and, though Caroline had lost one child, she grew more content now that her relationship with the other two was secure at last.

In 1840 Caroline published *The Dream and Other Poems*, the volume which so delighted Hartley Coleridge, and during the next several years she worked at her most ambitious poem, *The Child of the Islands*. Like Hartley Coleridge, an anonymous reviewer of *The Dream* in R. H. Horne's *A New Spirit of the Age* (1844) compared Caroline with Elizabeth Barrett. He found her to be superior to Miss Barrett in her powers of construction, and he gave unstinting praise to Caroline's "great mental energies" and to her "beautifully clear and intelligible" verse, written "from the dictates of a human heart in all the eloquence of beauty and individuality."[2] Also during 1840 Caroline was received at court. She soon forgave Melbourne for his part in her former exclusion from the presence of the queen, and with that old source of irritation removed, their relationship resumed much of its former affection.

After his resignation in August, 1841, Melbourne felt isolated and abandoned. In 1843 he suffered a stroke, and by the time of Caroline's last three extant letters to him, he had retired to Brocket. At thirty-six, Caroline had regained her self-confidence and her social equilibrium, as well as her sons, and she was able to write to her old friend in a manner which reveals her pity for his infirmities and which is, at the same time, retentive of that sportive, teasing intimacy which marked their happiest days together.

163

1. Quoted by Acland, *Caroline Norton,* p. 132.
2. R. H. Horne, ed., *A New Spirit of the Age,* 2:139–40.

45

St. Leonards on Sea. [*November 1844*]

How can you turn such a deaf ear, and such a turned up nose, —
to the claims of old Jack Morris?[1] Why dont you help the man
that helped your brother at Westminster? in the good old days,
when *you* wasn't weak & sick, & *he* wasn't faint & starving? Do
you think the God who made Jack Morris & you, does not judge
it as selfishness? Something also perhaps of ingratitude? For no
doubt when he had his riches, & his 20 stall stable, & his
Westminster votes, very civil words you all said to him! O!
rouse your sluggish old heart to write to some one for him: and
dont fly in the face of Heaven who built up your own face into the
picture of honesty & generosity thereby (alas!) creating much
mistaken trust, & vain expectation, in the hearts of all those
whose ill-jud[g]ing eyes have gazed on your countenance.

Why dont you write? Who have you got at Brocket? Does
Emily[2] hang her long gowns up, like banners of Victory, in the
cupboards? Does *Sow's Body* sit there, talking ill of you to
Pig's face?[3] Does Lady Holland[4] *cut herself in four,* to help &
serve you? Are Fanny Jocelyn's[5] soft purple eyes at your table
under the lamp? or does the "Minny"[6] who rivals our "Georgy"
rouse you to any love & admiration of your own relations?

Send us a line, oh! Hoy.

My Secretary wrote me word that Pembroke had "discovered
Scheffer's depravity."[7] The Secretary is so extremely shocked,
that it is difficult to gather any connected history from his broken
ejaculations of sorrow & shame for an erring brother's conduct,

165

— & the dancer's irregularities, — (and indeed *'tis* shameful that good dancers should make false steps so often) but it seems there has been a row. My Secretary is too intellectual to get into those sort of scrapes. Love be damned, as an idle vagabond boy, is our motto, and that is a great satisfaction.

As to Pembroke, who never discovers the Lady's "depravity" till he is tired of her, — and then chuses [*sic*] another, — on the good Royal principle of "the Reigning Ballet Dancer never dies" — I can't say I feel any great pity for him. Next year there will be another fracas, & so on to the end of his life, but a shadow of sorrow for the poor little intriguing wench herself, comes over me, as meanwhile she is to endure "the great pain & peril of Childbirth" without any present prospect of a pitying Father to pay the Nurse or own the baby.

Lizst [*sic*], the Pianiste, once said that people to whom God had given a great genius for anything, ought not to think of *love,* and truly the last genius that should think of the sort of love that ends in a lying-in is a dancer. She ought to flutter through the world like a Sylph, — & never rest.

Adieu. I am extremely busy, yet I write to you. You are not busy, yet you do not write to me. I abjure the world — & will sell all I have & give to the Poor.

Tomorrow is Brin's birthday & we have ordered Roast Pig for dinner.

> God bless you,
> Ever yrs
> *Car*

1. Sir John Morris, second baronet (1775–1855).

2. According to Acland (*Caroline Norton,* p. 161), the reference is to Melbourne's great-niece, the daughter of Emily, Lady Ashley and the seventh earl of Shaftesbury.

3. Most likely Mrs. Norton had no one in particular in mind. Her language is expressive of her general distaste for the women among Melbourne's friends and relatives.

4. Elizabeth, Lady Holland (1770–1845), the unconventional wife of Henry Richard Fox, third baron Holland; queen of the Whig aristocracy and hostess at Holland House to the cream of the London *haut ton* for more than four decades. Lady Holland was renowned as an arbiter of fashion and as a caustic wit, and she once tore a wreath of roses from Caroline Norton's head with, "There, *now* you look decent; those roses were quite out of keeping with your style" (Marjorie Villiers, *The Grand Whiggery,* p. 247). Some years later, in a more charitable mood, she described Mrs. Norton to her son, Henry Edward Fox, in a letter dated June 30, 1840: "She is in greater beauty if possible than ever, but very cross & touchy they say. She expected her reception at Court would open all arms & doors to her. Not finding this or much beyond great civility for routs & balls, she is angry" (Holland, *Elizabeth, Lady Holland To Her Son, 1821–1845,* pp. 187–88).

5. Formerly Lady Fanny Cowper.

6. Melbourne's niece, Lady Ashley, whose beauty Caroline compared to that of Georgiana, Lady Seymour. (See above, Letter 6, n. 3.)

7. Robert Henry Herbert, twelfth earl of Pembroke and ninth earl of Montgomery (1791–1862), had as mistress the popular ballet dancer Elisa Scheffer, best remembered for appearances at Her Majesty's Theatre during the seasons of 1843 and 1844. For a brief time Pembroke also enjoyed the favors of Adeline Plunkett, another dancer at Her Majesty's who was Scheffer's implacable enemy. During a performance of *Ondine,* on the evening of May 11, 1844, the two quarreled openly and savagely on stage, and not long thereafter they were dismissed. A few months later, when Pembroke fell ill, his friends attempted to rescue the earl from Scheffer's thrall by persuading him that his illness had resulted from a love philtre supposedly administered secretly by Scheffer and her mother. Bewildered and distressed by these accusations, Pembroke withdrew to Paris in the late autumn. But Scheffer pursued him, and they were soon reconciled. Her career was quite forgotten in her happy concubinage, and she lived with Pembroke in Paris until his death, bearing him three children.

Pembroke's eminent son, Sidney Herbert, first baron Herbert of Lea (1810–1861), was Caroline Norton's frequent companion for several years prior to his marriage in 1849.

46

St. *Leonard's-on-Sea*
6th Dec^r [1844]

Dearest old Boy, pray do write. I am ill in bed myself and if you don't write, I shall think you are *ill in bed too*.

I did imagine I had coaxed you into scribbling by asking you that information for my poem.[1] You always say you are glad to teach me things and supply me with scraps of knowledge. How shall I get on if I am so neglected by my Tutor?

The boy's [*sic*] Tutor, whose name is Mr. Murray[2] and who is Curate here, is the first gentleman of Scotch extraction I ever met who knew nothing whatever about his Clan or his family. In general they will ferret you out their Roots, (to say nothing of their Branches), with the sagacity of trufle dogs: but here's a fellow who asks what Dunmore's[3] title is, and *who* is the elder branch of the Murray Clan! There is a passage in my Poem about the Church disturbances in Scotland, against those who want to elect their own minister.[4] Breadalbane[5] wanted me to leave it out, but I have been obstinate. I told him what you had said about the difference between being *in* and *out* of office: he laughed very much and said he should send you a *whole Deer* to make up.

Do write to me! I do not ask it altogether out of selfishness. I am sure if you dont write to me — you do *nothing:* and that is very bad for you. See now, I have written to *you*, tho' I am in bed, with leeches for my *Pillow-Fellows*. (I call them *Pillow-Fellows* because *Bedfellows* take up more room.)

God bless you.
Ever Yrs
Caroline

1. *The Child of the Islands*, which Caroline addressed to the young Prince of Wales (ultimately Edward VII). As Caroline explained in the "Preface," the long poem was designed not as a birthday ode or an address of congratulation, but rather as a multifarious piece treating the birth of the prince as a harbinger of a return to innocence and good will in all spheres of British life. The poem suggests that a common response of affection for the royal child will inspire a feeling of gentle concord throughout the land and that one day discrimination and deprivation will be as foreign to children of every grade and class as they are to the infant Prince of Wales.

2. James Murray, who subsequently became curate of St. Stephen's, Norwich, and, in the early 1850s, perpetual curate of St. Giles, Norwich.

3. Alexander Edward Murray, sixth earl of Dunmore and first duke of Cambridge (1804–45); he succeeded to the Dunmore title in 1836.

4. In May, 1843, a sizeable branch of the Scottish Church seceded from the Presbytery to form an autonomous church responsible for its own regulation, including the local selection of its ministers. Caroline Norton pictured the Scottish religious agitators as disgraceful malcontents in "Autumn," section three of *The Child of the Islands*.

5. John Campbell, second marquess of Breadalbane (1796–1862), styled Viscount Glenorchy until 1831, when he became Breadalbane. He was M.P. for Okehampton from 1820 till 1826, and in 1832 he was elected to represent Perthshire.

47

I am glad the interest of your gates[1] made you write directly —
but you disturbed yourself unnecessarily. I have no enthusiasms
which make me forget what you say to me, and you told me at
the time all that you have taken the trouble to write per post. If
you had *read*, as carefully as I *listen*, you would have seen that
in my letter I mention having been promised *designs*, and that I
merely repeat the observations of *others* when I talk of Baldock[2]
and his triumphal entries.

It has since struck me that as the place is in fact Mrs. Lamb's[3]
(and probably also the projected improvement), her leisure
would be well employed, and her taste better satisfied by chos-
ing [*sic*] them herself.

Mrs. Stanhope[4] does not care about politics for the best of all
reasons, which is that she cannot by any effort be brought to
comprehend them, even in the shallow way we women do: She
takes them as Helen does (only that Helen *could* understand
them) and [Ariel's?][5] way I will recount. I got a long letter from
the Beau[6] that time that I was so provoked & anxious at Paris.
Helen was ill in bed, I thought the Beau's epistle might amuse
her & took it accordingly. She put out one hand in a languid
deprecating manner, and said, "dont look so eager Caroline, and
above all things dont read it to me if there *are any politics in it*,
for I know I shall be bored & tried to death."—

As to Leicester Stanhope you are wrong if you think him
stupid. He may be wrongheaded, but he is a fine spirited

creature full of information tho' habitually silent; and those who are not against you *may be* with you. Mrs. S.[tanhope] has a number of set phrases of the "jobbing" of the Whigs, & the "dishonesty" of the Whigs, &c &c, but neither for the past nor for the present has she a definite idea. She told Lady Harrington *before Lord H.*[7] that Mr. Claggett[8] said he could have had her on his own terms; & on Leicester interposing, she said, *"You know you told me so yourself."* This has made a family quarrel & she is not yet convinced it was a foolish thing to do.

Georgia has sent for me to sit with her as she is ill & low — so farewell.

Yrs ever, Car.

1. Melbourne had evidently undertaken some remodeling at Brocket Hall.

2. Edward Holmes Baldock (1812–75), M.P. for Shrewsbury from 1847 until 1857.

3. Probably the reference is to Melbourne's sister-in-law, Lady Beauvale (Mrs. Frederick Lamb), the former Countess von Mahltzahn, daughter of the Prussian envoy to the court of Vienna. After their marriage in February, 1841, Lord Beauvale and his wife were periodic residents at Brocket Hall until his death in 1853. In 1848, at his brother's death, Beauvale became third viscount Melbourne.

4. Elizabeth Stanhope (d. 1898), the only child and heir of William Green of Jamaica and wife of Caroline's dear friend, Colonel Leicester Stanhope (see above, Letter 19, n. 1).

5. Probably Caroline's nickname for Helen, Lady Dufferin. Perkins transcribes the name as "Nell" (*Mrs. Norton,* p. 200).

6. Arthur Wellesley, first duke of Wellington (1769–1852).

7. Charles Stanhope, fourth earl of Harrington (1780–1851), major-general, was the elder brother of Colonel Leicester Stanhope, who succeeded to the title upon the fourth earl's death. Lady Harrington (d. 1867) was the former Maria Foote.

8. Unidentified.

Bibliography

Acland, Alice. *Caroline Norton*. London: Constable, 1948.

Airlie, Mabell, Countess of. *Lady Palmerston and Her Times*. 2 vols. London: Hodder and Stoughton, 1922.

Brookfield, Charles, and Brookfield, Frances. *Mrs. Brookfield and Her Circle*. London: Isaac Pitman and Sons, 1905.

Bulwer, Victor, Earl of Lytton. *The Life of Edward Bulwer, First Lord Lytton*. London: Macmillan, 1913.

Carlyle, Jane Welsh. *Jane Welsh Carlyle: Letters to Her Family, 1839–1863*. Edited by Leonard Huxley. London: John Murray, 1924.

Cecil, David. *Lord M.: Or the Later Life of Lord Melbourne*. London: Constable, 1954.

Douglas, George. *George Douglas, Eighth Duke of Argyll: Autobiography and Memoirs*. Edited by the Dowager Duchess of Argyll. 2 vols. London: John Murray, 1906.

Dunckley, Henry. *Lord Melbourne*. London: Sampson, Low and Co., 1890.

Eden, Emily. *Miss Eden's Letters*. Edited by Violet Dickinson. London: Macmillan, 1919.

Granville, Harriet, Countess of. *Letters of Harriet Countess Granville, 1810–1845*. Edited by F. Leveson Gower. London: Oxford University Press, 1894.

Holland, Elizabeth. *Elizabeth, Lady Holland to Her Son, 1821–1845*. Edited by the Earl of Ilchester. London: John Murray, 1946.

Holland, Henry Edward Fox. *The Journal of the Honourable Henry Edward Fox, 1818–1830*. Edited by the Earl of Ilchester. London: T. Butterworth, 1923.

Horne, R. H., ed. *A New Spirit of the Age*. 2 vols. London: Smith, Elder and Company, 1844.

[Kemble, John.] "Custody of Infants Bill." *British and Foreign Review* 7 (1838): 269–411.

Killham, John. *Tennyson and The Princess*. London: Athlone Press, 1958.

Litchfield, Henrietta, ed. *Emma Darwin: A Century of Family Letters*. 2 vols. London: John Murray, 1915.

Newman, Bertram. *Lord Melbourne*. London: Macmillan, 1930.

Norton, Caroline. *The Dream; and Other Poems*. New York and Boston: C. S. Francis and Co., 1849.

Olney, Clarke. "Caroline Norton to Lord Melbourne." *Victorian Studies 8* (March, 1965) :255–62.

———. *"Glenarvon* Revisited." *University of Kansas City Review* 22 (1955): 271–76.

Perkins, Jane Gray. *The Life of the Honourable Mrs. Norton*. New York: Henry Holt, 1909.

Pierce, Edward L. *Memoir and Letters of Charles Summer*. 4 vols. Boston: Roberts Brothers, 1877.

Richardson, Joanna. *My Dearest Uncle: A Life of Leopold, First King of the Belgians*. London: Jonathan Cape, 1961.

Roberts, R. Ellis. *Samuel Rogers and His Circle*. New York: E. P. Dutton and Co., 1910.

Robinson, Henry Crabb. *Henry Crabb Robinson on Books and Their Writers*. Edited by Edith J. Morley. 3 vols. London: J. M. Dent and Sons, 1938.

Sadlier, Michael. *Bulwer: A Panorama: Edward and Rosina, 1803–1836*. London: Constable, 1931.

Thackeray, William Makepeace. *The Letters and Private Papers of William Makepeace Thackeray*. Edited by Gordon N. Ray. 4 vols. Cambridge, Mass.: Harvard University Press, 1945–46.

Trelawney, Edward John. *Letters of Edward John Trelawney*. Edited by H. Buxton Forman. London: Oxford University Press, 1910.

Torrens, William M. *Viscount Melbourne*. London, New York, and Melbourne: Ward, Lock and Co., 1890.

Villiers, Marjorie. *The Grand Whiggery*. London: John Murray, 1939.

Index

176

Lyndhurst, Lord, 19 n.14
Lytton, Edward Robert (later Lord Lytton), 150 n

Mackintosh, James, 25, 26 n
Maginn, William, 19 n.16
Maiden Bradley, 25, 26, 26 n, 42, 50, 86 n, 125
Marlborough House, 53
Marryat, Frederick, 134, 135 n
Martineau, Harriet, 14, 15
Mavrocordatos, Prince Alexander, 85 n
Medea, 117 n
Meek, Ellen, 84
Melbourne, Lord (William Lamb): meets Caroline, 6; assists George Norton, 6–7; and Lady Branden, 7, 19 n.10, 21 n.31, 63, 83, 92, 93, 120; characteristics of, 7, 60; his need for Caroline, 7, 62; amorous reputation of, 9; trial of (1836), 9–10, 79–98 passim, 98 n, 125, 134, 135 n, 144, 146, 151; acquittal of, 10, 80; at Brocket Hall, 16, 61, 163, 165, 170, 171 n; visits Caroline at her uncle's home, 16, 130; death of, 17, 21 n.31; and Disraeli, 19 n.13; and Lord Brougham, 19 n.14; makes bequest to Caroline, 21 n. 31, 132 n; and his ward Susan, 28–30, 31, 31 n, 32, 39–40, 51; attends opening of London Bridge, 32, 38 n, 39; and Emily Eden, 42–43, 44 n; health of, 50, 74 n, 163; second ministry of, 62; fears scandal, 63; his letters to Caroline, 63, 74 n, 91, 98, 104, 112, 114, 154; discourages communication with Caroline, 63, 91, 100, 102, 104–5, 110, 112, 124–25, 127, 128; offers to resign, 79; backs Irish Municipal Corporations Bill, 107, 109 n; and Lady Stanhope, 117 n, 120, 122, 133, 142–49 passim; sends flowers to Caroline, 138, 141, 142; and Queen Victoria, 145, 148, 150 n, 161 n; mentioned, 3, 11–17 passim, 44 n, 45 n, 51 n, 58 n, 69 n, 78 n, 86 n, 88 n, 108, 119 n, 123 n, 129 n, 129 n, 135 n. See also Norton, Caroline Sheridan, Melbourne relationship; Norton, George, his suit against Melbourne
Melbourne, Viscountess, 7
Menzies, Lady, 11, 91, 132 n
Menzies, Sir Neil, 11, 162

Meredith, George, 3, 4, 16; Diana of the Crossways, 18 n.1
Middle Temple, the, 37, 38 n
Millbank Prison, 52, 54 n
Minto, Lady, 116, 117 n, 122
Minto, Lord, 117 n
Moore, Mrs. (the nurse), 84
Moore, Thomas, 5, 18 n.6; "Summer Fête," 18 n.6
Morpeth, Lady, 20 n.28
Morris, Sir John, 165, 166 n
Murray, James, 168, 169 n
Murray, John, 110, 144

Napier, Lord, 31 n, 52
Napier, Miss (the schoolgirl), 39
Napier, Sir William Francis, 41 n
Nemours, duc de, 55 n
Normanby, Lord, 160, 161 n
Norton, Augusta, 8, 13
Norton, Brinsley (son): birth of, 6, 41 n; death of, 21 n.32; abused by father, 108; favored by Caroline, 130, 132 n; mentioned, 64, 79, 84, 142, 163, 166. See also Norton, Caroline Sheridan, Children
Norton, Caroline Sheridan (1809–77)
—appearance: eyes, 3, 18 n.8, 30; Linley beauty, 3. See also Norton, Caroline Sheridan, Descriptions by contemporaries, Descriptions of herself
—characteristics: her social behavior, 3, 4, 5, 9, 15, 18 n.6, 20 n.28; her disposition, 3, 5, 6, 7, 9, 15, 17, 20 n.28, 56; her talents, 3, 5, 15, 21 n.28; her intelligence, 3, 5, 18 n.8, 26 n.1. See also Norton, Caroline Sheridan, Appearance, Descriptions by contemporaries, Descriptions of herself
—children, 6, 77, 95, 95 n, 97, 112, 146; efforts to gain access to, 8, 15, 67–68; 110, 136, 144, 151–52, 154, 162; her anguish over, 11–13, 64–65, 73, 91, 105, 108–9; on governing, 56; her love for, 57, 72, 75, 130, 132 n; endeavors to steal, 79; meets by stealth, 91; visits with, 137, 140, 142, 143 n, 153 n; her ultimate access to, 163. See also Norton, Brinsley; Norton, George; Norton Fletcher Spencer; Norton, William

—descriptions by contemporaries: Emily, Lady Cowper, 3; Lord Holland, 4; Charles Sumner, 5; William Brookfield, 11; John Kemble, 14, 20 n.27; William Makepeace Thackeray, 18 n.8; Jane Welsh Carlyle, 19 n.8; William Maginn, 19 n.16; duchess of Sutherland, 20 n.23; Alfred, Lord Tennyson, 20 n.27; Harriet, Lady Granville, 20 n.28; Fanny Allen, 20–21 n.28; Elizabeth, Lady Eastlake, 21 n.28; Emily Eden, 44 n; William Melbourne, 63; Mary Shelley, 78 n; Edward John Trelawny, 135 n; Elizabeth, Lady Holland, 167 n

—descriptions of herself: her appearance, 30, 50, 51, 53, 131, 152; her vanity, 53; her defiance, 56; as wife, 89; her restlessness, 120

—friends and advisors: Sidney Herbert, 17, 167 n; William Stirling-Maxwell, 17; Henry Taylor, 27 n; the Charles Nortons, 48 n; Lord Seymour, 64, 65, 66 n, 67, 85, 107; Brinsley Sheridan, 65, 66 n, 72, 73, 95, 107, 152; Sir James Graham, 66 n, 67, 72, 81, 87, 88, 95, 102; Stephen Lushington, 74 n; Lord Lansdowne, 76 n; Mary Shelley, 78 n; the Leicester Stanhopes, 85 n; Mr. Bentick, 88 n; Edward Ellice, 123 n

—marriage, 11, 12, 15–16, 59–60, 110; sources of animosity in, 4–6; responds to Norton's character and behavior, 5, 8, 12–13, 65, 73, 77, 89, 94, 107–8, 114, 136, 140, 162; leaves Norton, 8, 62; agrees to return, 12, 136; Melbourne's advice concerning, 62–63, 87–88, 110; contemplates divorce and settlement possibilities, 67–68, 72, 85, 95, 100. *See also* Norton, Caroline Sheridan, Children; Norton, George

—Melbourne relationship, 43, 44–45 n, 62, 70, 85, 107, 138, 141, 142, 144, 151, 167 n; early days of, 6–8; public reaction to, 8–9, 60, 62, 63, 79; her love for Melbourne, 10, 17, 75–76, 83, 89, 93, 98; reproaches Melbourne, 16, 29–30, 63, 73, 75, 81, 83, 91, 95, 96–98, 102, 104–5, 110, 114–28 passim, 133, 134, 145–49 passim, 160–61, 165; reconciliation in, 16, 163; Melbourne's financial assistance to her, 21 n.31, 130, 132 n; asks Mel-

bourne to write, 50, 54, 64–65, 77, 95, 100, 102, 109, 119, 165, 168; her sadness and cynicism about, 68–69, 73, 75–76, 82, 90, 91–92, 93, 110–11, 112, 114, 121, 131, 143, 152–53; visits Melbourne, 82 n, 112; threatens Melbourne, 121, 147, 149; beseeches Melbourne to visit, 113, 121, 122, 124–25, 127, 131. *See also* Melbourne, Lord, trial of

—politics, 30, 107, 168, 169 n; campaigns for 1832 Reform Bill, 6; desires political influence, 6, 7–8; her Whig sympathies, 6, 12; Infant Custody Bill, 12, 13–15, 19 n.14, 110; responds to Kemble's charges, 14; and Lord Brougham, 19 n.14; on Leopold of Saxe-Coburg, 42, 49, 53

—social position, 11, 15, 59; acceptance in London society, 3, 5; her ruined reputation, 10–11, 96, 98, 155; troubled by exclusion from court, 16, 111, 144–45, 148–49, 149–50 n, 155, 160–61; and Lady Cowper, 128, 129 n, 133, 135 n; and Lady Stanhope, 133, 135 n; received at court, 163, 167 n

—works: "Plain Letter to the Lord Chancellor on the Infant Custody Bill, A," 15; *Dream, and Other Poems, The*, 20 n.23, 163; *Sorrows of Rosalie, The*, 39, 47; "On Seeing Anthony, the Eldest Child of Lord and Lady Ashley," 45 n; *Voice from the Factories, A*, 45 n, 110; "Separation of Mother and Child by the Custody of Infants Considered," 110; *Child of the Islands, The*, 163, 169 n

Norton, Charles, 47, 48 n, 52, 56, 61, 84, 85

Norton, Mrs. Charles, 48 n, 85

Norton, Fletcher Spencer (son): birth of, 6; death of, 21 n.32; health of, 52, 56–57, 64, 65 n; taken to lawyers, 109; mentioned, 58 n, 77, 108, 142, 163. *See also* Norton, Caroline Sheridan, Children

Norton, George: marries Caroline, 4; in parliament, 4; characteristics of, 4, 5, 8; is jealous of Caroline, 5, 8; cruelty of, 5, 8, 64–65, 68, 77, 107–8, 134, 144; political loyalties of, 6; his family interferes in marriage of, 6, 8, 13, 136; secures magistracy, 6–7, 116 n; accuses Caroline of adultery, 8; his suit

182